$1

PENGUIN BOOKS

"Dear Gangster …"

The Gangster of Love prefers to be known
only by his *nom de guerre*.

"DEAR GANGSTER..."

Advice for the Lonelyhearted from

The Gangster of Love

penguin books

PENGUIN BOOKS
Published by the Penguin Group
Penguin Books USA Inc., 375 Hudson Street, New York, New York 10014, U.S.A.
Penguin Books Ltd, 27 Wrights Lane, London W8 5TZ, England
Penguin Books Australia Ltd, Ringwood, Victoria, Australia
Penguin Books Canada Ltd, 10 Alcorn Avenue, Toronto, Ontario, Canada M4V 3B2
Penguin Books (N.Z.) Ltd, 182–190 Wairau Road, Auckland 10, New Zealand

Penguin Books Ltd, Registered Offices: Harmondsworth, Middlesex, England

First published in Penguin Books 1996

1 3 5 7 9 10 8 6 4 2

The contents of this book first appeared in the author's column in the
San Jose Mercury News's eye magazine.

LIBRARY OF CONGRESS CATALOGING IN PUBLICATION DATA
Gangster of Love.
Dear gangster—: advice for the lonelyhearted from The Gangster of Love.
p.   cm.
ISBN 0 14 02.4515 4 (pbk.)
1. Love—Humor.   2. Advice column—Humor.   I. Title.
PN6162.G22   1996
818'.5402—dc20   95–30551

Printed in the United States of America
Set in Berkeley Book
Designed by Claire Vaccaro

Contents

III.

Introduction
by Dave Barry

Who is The Gangster of Love?

I can't tell you.

Oh, I know him. I've known him for ten years. But I can't tell you who he really is. The Gangster has a secret identity, just like Superman, except that I never could understand why Superman *needed* a secret identify. I mean, he's *Superman*. What is he afraid of? That people will find out where he lives? That, some day when he's out fighting evil, people will break into his house and discover that The Man of Steel has a sticky area on his kitchen floor from when he spilled Smucker's grape jelly and just wiped it up with a dry paper towel because he was too lazy to get out the mop and the Mister Clean? That people will check out his CD collection and discover that he is deeply into Gary Puckett? That people will find stains on his sheets, or little hairs on his commode, or a giant tube of Preparation H in his medicine cabinet? Or maybe that, in his closet, he keeps a life-size inflatable doll that looks like Lois Lane? Or, God forbid, Jimmy Olsen? Is that what Superman is hiding from us?

And come to think of it, who, really, is Mister Clean?

I guess everybody has a secret side. The Gangster of Love definitely does, which is why I can't tell you his real name. For the record, he's not me. I'm a humor columnist; I deal with the easy, obvious, topics—politics, religion, life, death, exploding cows.

But The Gangster has no time for trivia. The Gangster writes about the only truly important topic, the Super Bowl of Topics, the King Kong of Topics, the Big Bang of Topics, the Young Mozart of Topics, the 32-ounce Prime Rib with Your Choice of Scalloped or Baked Potato of Topics, the Michael Jordan in his Physical Prime Taking Off with the Basketball from the Foul Line and Coming Down Several Minutes Later from the Rafters to JAM that Baby Home Over Three or Four Larger Defenders of Topics:

Love.

That's all that matters, in the end. To everybody. You tune in to CNN and you see a group of world leaders at some economic summit, standing around in their suits, emitting carefully worded remarks about the Japanese yen, and you may *believe* they're actually *thinking* about the world economy, but they're not, at least not deep inside, where the real thinking goes on. They're thinking . . .

Need to see her . . .
Afraid that he . . .
Does she think that I . . .
If he knew that I . . .
Please let her be . . .

Does he really . . .

How do I tell her that . . .

God do I want to . . .

Just like the rest of us. We're all emitting remarks from our mouths, but feeling something much more complicated, much stronger, much harder to talk about, in our gut. We're forever wrestling with the Big Strong Snake of Passion, which never stops writhing, so that no matter how many times we think we've finally got it permanently pinned in a hold it can't escape from (*Now, finally, I can stop worrying about this and get on with my REAL life*), it always puts a slithery new move on us, and suddenly it's *gone.* Or, worse, it has itself wrapped around us, and the harder we struggle (*No! I don't have TIME for this! I have to get my car inspected!*) the tighter it coils around us, and all we can think about is . . .

Need to see her . . .

Afraid that he . . .

Because the truth is that there is no other "real" life. Unless you're some kind of inhuman mutant reptilian George Steinbrennerish being, love, or the void you feel without it, *is* your real life. And it's not an easy life. As singer-poet Greg Brown says;

"It's easy to do the goat dance

But it's hard, it's so hard, to really love somebody."

The Gangster knows this. He knows this as well as anybody you've ever read. He knows the romantic moonlit I-just-met-this-person-ten-minutes-ago-and-already-I-know-that-I-want-us-to-get-married-and-have-a-minimum-of-twenty-three-children glory of love; he also knows the shameful, petty, greedy, pathetic, insecure, hateful, strew-the-bastard's-clothes-all-over-the-driveway-and-get-the-dog-to-pee-on-them disillusionment of love.

The Gangster knows this and more. He sees love from all the angles, angles you never thought of, angles you may be didn't *want* to think of, but that you'll be fascinated to read about nonetheless. The Gangster is like a way-hipper version of Dear Abby on sodium pentathol. People write to him with their questions, and he can't stop himself from answering with the truth, even when this is clearly the last thing they want. He doesn't give easy answers, because he knows there are none. The Gangster doesn't waste anybody's time with Seven Rules for a Successful Relationship, because he knows that love can turn sour over a package of Lifesavers.

The Gangster has looked into the Heart of Love's Darkness, and he's not afraid to talk about what he has seen.

You still want to know who the Gangster of Love is?

Start reading.

i

LIVE AT THE LIVIN' LARGE LOUNGE

Dear Gangster: *I was engaged and lived with the same person for four years but we've been split up now for about a year and a half. I didn't miss him but I couldn't get used to sleeping alone so . . . what I'm trying to say is, is it O.K. to like just fill the space with something, anything? . . . I mean substitute a . . .*

—Something, Anything

Dear Something, Anything: Listen, I don't know exactly what it is you're trying to tip-toe around but if you were bold enough to admit say, that for the past eighteen months all you've been sleeping with is a Teddy Ruxpin you picked up at a garage sale because you realized you can turn the volume off and his mouth still moves up and down in perfect rhythm, I would be the last person to judge you. I would suggest, however, that perhaps you turn the volume back up 'cause the guy does tell great stories.

Dear Gangster: *I met this great guy in Blockbuster Video and it really seemed that he had his heart in the right place, if you know what I mean. What does that mean, anyway? But listen, the thing is, he's only taken me out once (to The Olive Garden) and now it seems that all he wants to do is stay home and get drunk and watch these Christopher Walken movies that I've never even heard of. He sometimes watches the same ones over and over again for like forty-eight hours straight.* **—Walken all over Me**

Dear All Over: A. Dump him. B. Please send me his number.

Dear Gangster: *I feel funny about even asking you this because I know the answer but . . . this guy I've been seeing who's a pretty good guy has asked me to move in with him and it's just that I wish things were going smoother because I've only been working on and off lately and right now I'm in this crummy little place and he has a much bigger, nicer place but I don't want that to be the reason I move in—not that I'm the kind of person who would move in with somebody just for their place but it's so inviting that I keep questioning my motives. But then again I don't want to penalize him because he has a much better apartment than me and I don't want to jeopardize our whole relationship over something that I'm not even sure of and if he had a crummy little place like mine I'm not so sure I wouldn't still be hesitating, even though it wouldn't be about his place, it might be something else. I can't seem to make a decision because I don't think*

I'm capable of making an intelligent one while living in this crummy little place and waiting for something to happen in my life that's going to get me out. I don't know. Can you help me?
—Twice the Square Footage and an Almost View

Dear Twice the Square Footage Etc.: Yes, it's O.K. to move in with someone just because they have a nicer place. Half of us wouldn't be here today if people didn't do that. Only one out of eighteen people actually gets seriously involved with someone because of true love. The rest are due to bank balances, power positions, showbiz ties, and all those other things that lead to more square footage and better views. By accepting this invite you're actually helping the odds for the rest of us who are holding out for true love.

Dear Gangster: *I've only had two real loves in my life. The first was a troubled young woman. While her troubles at first seemed endearing—because I thought I could help—they eventually became our troubles. The second love was so much more stable and safe and so much more fulfilling than the first, I thought I'd never find a better situation if ever she decided to leave me. She did.*

I was right—it's been nearly a year and no one seems to measure up in comparison. Am I doomed to search eternally for the perfect woman, only to realize that I let her slip away? **—She Got Away**

Dear She Got: Only two real loves in your life? Yeah, it's over for you, especially since you started talking like a Jesuit priest ("The first was a troubled young woman") in a home for runaway teenagers. Two real loves? Give the rest of us a chance, will you, my son?

Dear Gangster: *My boyfriend's hooked on having sex in the kitchen. Sure, it was exciting at first but now it's so common that it's just about replaced the bedroom and I want my kitchen back. I want it to be the place where I prepare my meals again. Am I being a prude?*

—The Galloping Gourmet

Dear Galloping: Kitchen Smitchen. I know this couple that brags about doing it in an automatic car wash. They knew they wouldn't have much time so they got worked up in the car on the way over and at the first sight of thundering soap they jumped on the hood. "The bristles were dancing in every pore of my body," the guy said. "And when everything went white it was like being in Care Bear hell. So erotic." Luckily, before I started telling everybody they had to try this, the girlfriend gave me the other side of the story. "That one instance has ruined sex for us forever," she said. Seems they didn't get back in the car before the hot wax cycle and both got a sheen you wouldn't believe. "Weeks later I was still powdering my forehead like I was Telly Savalas," she said. But the worst of it was that this one sensational moment of sex has ruined good ol' fashioned regular sex forever. "We are both so waxed up we keep slipping off the bed and when we hit the floor we slide around the room like a couple of hockey pucks." Anyway, it gets worse: she ended up cracking two vertebrae when she slid into the family dog snoozing in the hallway. "Imagine how I felt at the hospital. Imagine having to tell them I had a head-on collision with a sleeping dog," she said. "So I couldn't. I told them it happened while having sex in a car wash. It was much more believable."

Dear Gangster: *My girlfriend tells me I've got to take a few lessons and butch up a little. Be a bit more like some of the tough guys on the big screen, learn how to handle myself.*

—Who Should I Emulate?

Dear Emulator: Movie tough guys are a joke, my friend. It goes back to John Wayne. And tell me if I'm wrong here, but how did guys like him get respect from guys like our fathers, who had been through World War II and Korea and things like the Depression? Here's a guy who's making a living by getting make-up powdered on his face, playing with toy guns, having someone yell "Action!" at him, and reciting lines just like in a little kiddy play. The whole act of being an actor automatically makes you the farthest thing from a man's man. How could you possibly be a tough guy in a business like this? I read somewhere the other day that Sean Connery is " . . . not to be messed with. Doesn't take crap from anybody." Don't make me laugh. He's in the movie business, who the hell's he scaring, David Geffen? Peter Guber? Meg Tilly? They always bring up these actors' pasts like before he became a thespian he was a cargo loader for the Royal Navy, or "Hey, Clint Eastwood used to dig ditches." Well, let me tell you something. I used to dig graves. I've been a shellfish harvester for God's sake, and I'm about as menacing as the late great Peter Allen. Although I do think I could scare the crap out of Jon Peters.

Dear Gangster: *I've got a serious problem. There are certain days when I can't seem to make contact with people and it's getting worse. It's not shyness really. There are just days I feel so distant and I can't seem to break out of myself. My boyfriend gets fed up with me because we have our own business and on these days I make him handle all the phone calls and customers. He says I freeze up on him. Is there a cure?*   **—Sister Freeze**

Dear Sis: It's going around. I sometimes work in a small office building and the other day on my way in I noticed someone had left their car lights on in the parking lot. It was one of those days I'm incapable of conversing with humans but I said to myself, I have to make some kind of announcement. I must. I didn't want someone to be on their way home to a loving family and, click, then she has to come creeping back in and ask that dreaded question, "Does anyone have any cables?" and then of course only one hand goes up and it belongs to the office pervert and it would all be my fault and. . . . Anyway, I watched her from the window to be sure the pervert didn't try anything. Not that I would have said anything anyway. Just know that this problem is not as uncommon as you may think. For reasons unknown there will be days you walk around shielding your face like you just killed your mother and network news cameras are zooming in. By the way, you ever reach the point where you can't even stay in line at a deli? You start to think when you blurt "rye bread" it's going to come out as some alien gibberish and the guy's going to glare back with that meat-slicing glint in his eyes. You know when they call out "Number twenty-seven!" and everyone looks around and then they repeat it but no one ever comes forward? That's us. We're the number twenty-sevens in this world and some days we just go hungry.

Dear Gangster: *I'm seventeen years old and the girl I'm after is a year younger. Now, why is it I want to go out with a sixteen-year-old girl but she wants to go out with a twenty-three-year-old guy who tends bar and has no future? I'm a forward on the basketball team, have a full scholarship coming, and I want to be an optometrist someday and this girl won't even give me a shot.*

—Teenager with a Future

Dear Teenager: There's something irresistible about twenty-three-year-old men with no future. They can get their teenage girlfriends into the Livin' Large Lounge and load 'em up on peppermint schnapps. They drive a car that gets repossessed on the third of every month. Oh, and they get these rooms they can pay for by the week that usually have a great ice machine rumbling right outside the door. The bad part is you can't take advantage of a spry young girl's attraction to all this until you turn twenty-three and toss all your ambitions aside. In the meantime, the one thing you never say to a sophisticated sixteen-year-old female who yearns to throw up mouthwash drinks and have the headlights of a tow truck blare in her face while she has sex to the hum of an ice machine is, "But Darlene, I'm going to be an optometrist someday!"

Dear Gangster: *My girlfriend is absolutely nuts. She's not speaking to me now because of something I did to her in a dream. I love her but this is too much, I'm sorry.*

— **She's Livin' in a Dream World**

Dear She's Livin' in a Dream World: And where the hell are you livin', my friend? I'm sick of people who won't accept the responsibility of showing up in someone else's dream. About four weeks ago, someone who I thought was a close friend and more, shows up in a dream of mine. One of those that takes place in your apartment so it's like a serious reality dreamscape, and first thing she does is come at me with this fire-blowing hair dryer and all the fireballs are shooting around the room and then they begin chasing each other and start forming into flaming circles and she's moving my furniture around and marking out a runway on the tile floor with my Mennen Speed Stick and then she pulls out a stopwatch and a starter pistol like she's going to time me hurdling through hoops of fire spit out by her drugstore blow dryer. Like I am supposed to do this on command to amuse her. *This*, from a woman who hadn't even called me in about six weeks and then just shows up in the middle of the night and pulls this crap. Did I mention she once told me she loved me? Well, I cut her out of my life on the spot—with an electric hedge trimmer that I plugged into my dog's nostrils.

Dear Gangster: *What is the one thing you demand from past lovers?*
—**A Past Lover**

Dear Past Lover: Stay out of my dreams.

Dear Gangster: *My best girlfriend is upset about her fiancé's bachelor party and I was wondering if it would be O.K. to have a combination bachelor/bachelorette party on the same night? We could do it at my place.* —**Everybody Will Be Happy**

Dear Everybody: Yeah, it's been done. I just want to caution you though 'cause I once attended one where one minute everything was beautiful (boring, in other words) and the next all hell had broken loose in the kitchen. Seems they had bought two of those anatomically correct cakes everyone thinks are so cute. One for the bride-to-be and one for the groom. Anyway, bachelor number one had apparently been drinking all day and, while the night was still young, somehow ended up in the kitchen forcing these two cakes to have sex with one another. Before you knew it the whole kitchen was packed like there was a cockfight going on. It was the messiest sex I've ever seen. Bachelorette number one was shaking violently from having to ask herself that terrifying question, "What kind of man forces two cakes to have sex?" and by the time it was over the kitchen was destroyed. It was a great party. Yeah, have it at your place.

Dear Gangster: *On the slim chance that I might find true love I was thinking about placing a personal ad, but I'm afraid to do it*

by myself. Is it proper to do it with a friend or something? Kind of a two girls looking for two guys thing. Or would that just make the odds worse?
                                                              —Odds Ads

Dear Odds: It depends what your definition of love is these days. One guy I know told me how he and a bunch of the boys decided to place a group ad that read: six professional men looking for six professional women. They ended up meeting six nurses in a pub. "You could hardly tell they were nurses," he said. "And the stench of the bar outweighed the hospital smell." Anyway, the nurses all had Wednesdays off and so did the guys. Believe it or not four of the couples have since married. I said to the guy, can that really be love? "I don't know," he said. "Who cares? They all have Wednesdays off." What happened to his nurse? "I got my day off switched. Had to drop her."

Dear Gangster: *What have you found to be the best distance for a restraining order?*
                                                     —Drawing the Lines

Dear Lines: I've had a lot of friends that go for the fifty-yard-line right away, but think about it? Half a football field. Would you even know they were there? I mean the best part about a restraining order is being able to spot the person creeping around so you can yell, "Back, you bastard!" And then you have to think about how good your throwing arm is. I have a friend who deliberately follows her ex to the grocery store and then pops out in aisle 4B, accuses him of tailing her, and starts nailing him with those heavy jars of mayo. "I have every right, I have every right," she screams. Of course she does. Who's gonna argue? She has a helluva arm and the bag boys think she's the greatest.

Dear Gangster: *I'm with this guy who keeps changing his tune about everything. It's like things just flow in and out of him and he has no set principles. At first I thought it was cool but now I can't pin him down about anything. It wasn't too long ago that he wanted to have a baby and now he says he thinks he wants to travel without me for a while and then maybe come back and give it another whirl. But that was yesterday. Will this type of guy ever stick to one tune?*

—Spinning, But Definitely in Love

Dear Spinning: People with those kind of attitudes are usually pretty interesting characters but I'd hate to be in love with one. I was just reading Joe Klein's biography of Woody Guthrie and your man with the ever changing tunes reminded me of a part in the book where Woody is working with a woman who keeps complaining that live he doesn't sing the songs anything like he does on the records. "Well," Woody said, "if I want to take a breath between verses, I play a few extra chords. And if I forget the lines and want to remember them, I play a few extra chords. And if I want to get up and leave town, I get up and leave town." And then he got up and left.

Dear Gangster: *Does anything go? I got this guy who will do anything to get me to go out with him and he's very honest about it. But so am I. I will never go out with him.*

—Nothing Is Going to Work, Ronnie

Dear Nothing Is: I got a buddy who's relentless. He was telling me the other day that a woman in his office (who he'd been hopelessly trying to make contact with on some level other than bookkeeping) asked him to do her a favor. "I thought this is it. Now, I'm the guy she comes to when she needs a favor so it's time to make a move." But he had to do the favor first. Seems she'd just had a nasty breakup with her boyfriend and wanted to get him back for cheating on her. "She told me the one thing he hated more than anything was someone smoking in his car," he said. But she couldn't stand to smoke so she wanted him to sit in the car and smoke a whole pack of cigarettes. "I told her I don't smoke either," he said. "For me," she said. "Smoke for me. I'll buy." So he sat in the car while she kept watch and smoked a whole pack. "Camels, no less," he said. "She can be very vengeful." Anyway, he figures he must be on the top of her list now so he goes to ask her out. "And she tells me she can't stand the sight of me. She feels terrible about doing it. And what kind of friend am I for not stopping her when the whole thing was just a crime of passion. Well, I'm the kind of friend that doesn't want to just be her friend so I try to play off that terrible thing. You know, we're two people that have done a terrible deed so we can only find solace in each other's arms. But she'll have none of it. And I'm getting pissed, I mean, I smoked for her. Camels." So what'd you do? I said. "I put my hand on her thigh." You what? "We've been going out for three weeks now."

Dear Gangster: *You ever hear someone say something that makes you immediately fall in love with them?* —**Who Said That?**

Dear Who Said That?: As a matter of fact I was at a party the other night and as I walked in the door a woman made immediate eye contact with me and said, "How many Baldwin brothers are there anyway? Quick. Quick." I laughed out loud. She kept a straight face and then turned away. I looked at her from behind and just became mesmerized. I wanted to be part of her life in any capacity she wished. I would have gladly taken the job of sitting beside her as she ate fruit and swallowing anything she discarded—apple cores, peach pits, grape branches. I would happily become nothing more than her kid sister. She could smack me around and steal stuff from my room and I'd still be there at midnight to brush her hair one hundred strokes before she went to bed. I've always wanted a big sister anyway. And at that moment she owned me.

Now, the thing is, I was only at the party to get some keys from someone so I headed right back toward the door after I got them. She turned to me again as I passed. "Hey," she said. "How many Baldwin brothers are there anyway? Quick. Quick." And immediately everything changed. All of a sudden I wished she could have been shrunk and recast in solid iron and used as a foot scraper in the foyer of some Republican senator's home in Maryland where the mud always freezes to your shoes.

Dear Gangster: *If a man is absolutely fantastic at making love to you does that mean he loves you?* **—Not That it Matters**

Dear Not That: Here's a co-worker who let me in on what he thinks is an inside joke: "Hah, she thinks I can't get enough of her. She's been telling me how great I'm getting. She thinks it's her. She thinks I'm obsessed with every inch of her. She's got to be kidding. I'm just using her to practice on."

Dear Gangster: *We come up with a lot of obvious differences between men and women but what is the main one?*
—Counting on You

Dear Counting: I think it was a comic from Louisiana I shared a cab with once who told me the only real difference is that women even look sexy in men's clothing (flannel shirts were his favorite) but men never look sexy in women's clothing. At least, not to him.

Dear Gangster: *Can love really end?*

—**Just Wondering**

Dear Wondering: No, but it can be killed off and visited (at your convenience), once or twice a year, like the grave site of a distant relative, say a great-aunt or someone else you've only seen pictures of. We'll talk about this more next week.

Dear Gangster: *I've been engaged five times and each time I'm the one who calls off the engagement. I don't think it's because I'm scared. I think it's just that the men aren't good enough for me.*

—**Too Good to Be Wrong**

Dear Too Good: Is it you or everyone else? To me five times is a lot. But I had an associate who went through six wedding dates with six different men. "I grew up in a fairy tale. My father was a prince," she always said, "and all these fantasy men I get mixed up with turn into real people and then things fall apart." Now she's thirty-six and says that once romance betrays you too many times you give up on it, just like anything that fails time and time again. I saw her the other day and she said, "I'm a practical girl now. I'm looking for more of a brother than anything else, I guess. The people you love screw you over. I'm just gonna look for someone to have children with." So you see she hasn't changed her expectations but instead repackaged them in her head into something she thinks will work and, most importantly, she can live with. The only thing missing will be love.

Dear Gangster: *Is it really that important for two people to have the same sense of humor if they're going to have a lasting relationship?*

—**Funny Bones**

Dear Bones: "If she doesn't have the same sense of humor she just won't get me," my chiropractor says. But this guy goes to extremes. He insists women take what he calls the "laugh-track" test before he'll go out with them. The test consists of him and the woman watching *Seinfeld* in separate rooms while their reactions are recorded. After the show, he puts the two hand held recorders side by side and if every snicker, every sigh, every belly laugh isn't in synch she's dismissed. So far no one has passed.

Dear Gangster: *My fiancé's friends are planning a wild bachelor party for him. I don't want to be a prude but I have this feeling something awful is going to happen. Should I even say anything to him?*
—Just Got That Feeling

Dear JGTF: Prude. Although there was the time when the guy who makes duplicates of my keys got into a bit of trouble. His buddies took him out to one of those nudie bars where they have bachelor party specials. If I recall correctly the boys put together $120 so he could fight one of the "Foxy Boxing Troupe." Her name was Screech, I think. The club provided the boxing trunks and shaving cream for him to coat his body. He was then told to straddle the carpet. "Things got kind of blurry at this point," he said. "I was wiping off the cream when I heard this noise that sounded like a chimp in a blender (it was Screech) and all of a sudden I got a roundhouse kick in the mouth." Forty-four stitches. The wedding was the next morning. They had to have the wedding pictures airbrushed by the same guy who does Playboy. But the worst part was the pitiful fact that a working man, a key-making, born in Pittsburgh and relocated to sunny California kind of man, had to go on his honeymoon with no lips. But that's a one in a million incident. Tell your man to have a good time and kiss him one last time to be on the safe side.

Dear Gangster: *I'm sitting on my front porch doing I don't know what. Last night I went out with the girl who lives directly across the street for the first time. I had a lot of fun so I said, "You wanna do something tomorrow?" She said, "Sure." I said, "I'll call you tomorrow." She said, "No, no, don't call. Just come on over when you see some signs of life over here." Now I'm sitting here waiting for some kind of sign. It's chilly, so I don't think the windows are going to suddenly fly open and she's not the type to crank up the rider mower first thing. I ask you, what am I waiting for? How did I end up a man sitting on his porch waiting for signs of life?*   **—Sitting**

Dear Lifewatch: There's something very profound about all this. I saw a girl once who gave me the same line and all I had to go on was this apartment door on the floor below me. I kept creeping up to it, waiting for a shadow to pass the crack of light beneath the door. I even put my palms on it as if I'd be able to feel the heat from her Mr. Coffee. I listened for the sound of a hairbrush hitting the morning snares. I sniffed. Would the scent of mint dental floss signify life and give my knock the confidence it needed? I never saw her again, my friend. It was like she ceased to exist. I still pass by that old apartment building and wonder if she's there in a self-induced coma for fear that if she comes to life I will appear at her door. Could I do that to someone? There's something very profound about all this.

Dear Gangster: *Why is it when a woman turns me down for a date she has to give me a reason that usually hurts my feelings. The other day I asked a woman out and she said, "No thanks. I don't date egomaniacs." Now, why did she have to say that? Why not just say "No thanks" and let that be the end of it?*

—Don't Want No Reasons

Dear DWNR: Yeah, what's wrong with just saying, "No thanks?" These days you ask somebody if they want a cup of coffee and they say, "No thanks. I don't drink coffee." You wanna grab a hot dog? "No thanks. Don't you know they're made out of recycled newspapers taken from the bottoms of kennel cages?" Wanna wash your hair in my sink? "No thanks, I'd just as soon use Pssst, the dry shampoo for the bedridden, before I'd set foot in your bathroom." Would you like to accompany me to dinner and a show? "No thanks, you remind me of an uncle of mine who used to stick his head under old women's shower stalls at campgrounds in national parks." God Almighty, I think I'm speaking for everyone when I say, reasons serve no purpose. "No thanks" will do.

Dear Gangster: *My fiancé is rich, rich, rich and I'm lucky to have him and his money. The only irritating thing about him is that he's into all kinds of wild stuff like mountain climbing and scuba diving. I don't like those kinds of things but I also don't like being treated like a prude every time he introduces me to someone. It's like, "And this is my fiancée, she's my complete opposite. The stay at home when it's raining type." "Oh, she'll make a good wife," people say. What they mean is I'd make a good ottoman. How do I get him to stop?*

—Not So Dull Donna

Dear Not So Dull: I get it. "Meet Donna, she's not as adventuresome as me. She's not as outdoorsy as me." Just let the daredevil have his fun. Encourage him. "Why don't you try racing hydroplanes, hon? You'd look handsome in one of those acrobatic planes with a scarf flapping in the breeze. Why don't you go a little deeper on your next dive, Sweetheart?" With him involved in all these activities just think how easy it will be to kill him off and call it an accident. Everyone will say, "So sad, but he left doing what he loved best—being outdoorsy." And you'll be the rich, rich, richest ottoman in town.

Dear Gangster: *A dream is destroying me. My guy had always wanted to have his own restaurant someday. Well, we finally opened a place only to have to go out of business nine months later. Now he's working day and night for a catering place so he can try again. He won't let up and it's tearing us apart. I don't want to go through the whole thing again but what else can I do?*
—Dreams Live Hard

Dear Dreams Live Hard: You got that right. I want to give the guy credit for not giving up but I know how you feel. Dreams can wipe you out. Sometimes I think if you could just shut them down life would be a lot easier. I can't tell you how many people I've seen wasted by their own dreams. But will there ever be a cure? A dream vaccine? I hope not.

Dear Gangster: *My parents are both retired and in their early seventies. They have taken a real disliking to my boyfriend and say it makes them ill to see me with such a "shifty character." We're about to announce our engagement and I'm seriously afraid the news might literally kill them.*   **—My Finger's on the Trigger**

Dear Trigger: Just the opposite. This will give them something to live for. They'll be able to dwell and harp on every one of his faults from sunrise to sunset. It'll be what gets them out of bed every morning. I wouldn't be surprised if your marrying this "shifty character" adds fifteen to twenty years to their life expectancies. Invite me to your old man's one hundredth birthday party.

Dear Gangster: *I had a great island romance with a wonderful Greek goddess last year. We haven't seen each other since but vowed to meet in the same exact spot on the same stretch of beach again this October. I'm about to make my plane reservations. Do you think I'm getting my hopes too high?* **—Greek Expectations**

Dear Expectations: What are you doing to yourself? I know a guy who set the same kind of date after a glorious interlude with a woman in Jamaica. He thought about nothing else the entire year. When I drove him to the airport he was wearing a ridiculous straw hat with his heart stapled to it. Never saw him again. Last I heard he was working over there in some kind of freaky sideshow, next to a parasail booth, where he wrestles jellyfish in a submerged cage. But yeah, go ahead, catch your flight. I hear the pay's great.

Dear Gangster: *My girl has a more prestigious job and makes more money than me. It's not so much the money as the attitude she has about it. At first she acted cocky and kidded about it but I don't take it as kidding anymore.*

—What's So Funny about Money and Power?

Dear Inferior: You got a point there, man. But let me tell you what an old roommate of mine does. He's in the same position now and what he's done is reverted back to his childhood. "When I was a kid I always swiped change off my father's bureau and it somehow made it easier to swallow all the crap he was always giving me," he says. "Whenever he'd really get on my nerves I'd just jingle jangle those coins in my pocket and go buy an ice-cream soda on him. I've started doing the same thing with my wife's loose change. She can have the power. I'm going to the arcade."

Dear Gangster: *I was sitting up late last night writing down the attributes of my ideal man. It went something like this: 1. Dark eyes and a deep soul. 2. A relentless hunger for truth. 3. Love for all mankind no matter what. 4. Strong, but peaceful at heart. 5. Average in ways that are really noticeable, above average in ways that are barely noticeable. 6. Animal instincts that fit the human spirit. 7. A lover who could really touch a person. As soon as I finished I ripped it up into a million pieces. It's hopeless, isn't it? How could a man like that exist?*
                                                                    —The Shredder

Dear Shredder: I've only got two words for you on your way back to the wastebasket—"Billy Jack."

Dear Gangster: *I'm a little worried. My fiancé never seems to be able to follow through on anything, everything is half-assed. He seems to just get started on something and then he stops and is off to something else. I don't know if I can spend the rest of my life like this.*
                                                                    —The Other Half

Dear Other Half: I bet your engagement ring is half a karat. Listen, I have this buddy who has never finished anything. I once went shopping with him when he wanted to set up an aquarium. We were out all day but all he bought were fish. He couldn't decide on what size tank he wanted. When I left him he said he'd get it the next day. I stopped by the next week and there were all these fish still sitting around the house in baggies. When I harassed him about it he claimed he's lived an entire life in a half a lifetime. "I can start so many more things than the average person if I never finish anything," he said proudly. "Like raising goldfish on furniture?" I asked. "For one," he replied. You can't reason with a guy like that. But anyway, why on earth would you assume there's actually going to be a wedding?

Dear Gangster: *This guy is getting out of my house! I just haven't figured out how yet. Should I heap his clothes out on the front lawn? Should I change the locks while he's at work? I have to do it now while I've got my nerve up.*   **—My Boots Are On**

Dear Boots: Just don't do what my scandalous neighbor did. Her beau kept stepping out on her so she got real bold and decided to replace him while he was out one night. "What a shocker it'll be," she bragged to me that morning. She had arranged to borrow her boss's husband and pawn him off as her new guy. Her beau would stumble in and come face to face with her new man. His replacement. "He'll freak," she giggled. "I'll be sitting in this guy's lap guzzling a bottle of wine." Well, I don't know what went down that night, maybe it was the wine, but she got fired from her job and the three of them are now living together. I heard they're looking for a "smaller place."

Dear Gangster: *I've been seeing this one girl for almost four months now and we're getting along really well. The only problem is that she's been burned in her last few relationships and wants to keep me hidden from her friends and family in case it happens with me. She says she couldn't handle the embarrassment again. I tell her I feel like she's embarrassed by me or something. I want to be part of her entire life. When will I be able to come out of hiding?*   **—Extremely Low Profile**

Dear Low Pro: Either when men start giving women the respect they should never have had to earn and their hearts are massaged by men who are able to commit to love in a way that chains it to their souls forever, or when you dump her.

Dear Gangster: *I'm still in shock. After going together for a year and a half the guy I thought was the one dropped the bomb on me* *that he was moving three thousand miles away to try and win back his high-school sweetheart. He's twenty-four years old. How can he even know what this girl is doing now?* **—College Sweetheart**

Dear Sweetheart: He's got that "Petite Little Doll I Left Back Home Syndrome." Believe me, he's been making calls. He's got spies out. Men don't take chances like that. He knows exactly what her situation is. He knows she just ended another relationship and is extremely vulnerable. He knows she's been getting a few in her at the local tavern and telling exaggerated stories about Spirit Week '85 and then her voice lowers when she mentions Ken and how they first touched each other with papier-mâché on their hands while building the sophomore float that turned out to look like a hunchbacked mermaid but was really just supposed to be a happy fish since the theme that year was "Happy Fish." And he probably knows he can catch her on any Sunday at the flea market dressed in a mothball-scented cheerleader skirt hawking mint condition 1987 J.F.K. High yearbooks. All conjecture aside, if nothing else, he definitely knows how much she weighs.

Dear Gangster: *They keep getting away. I met this great girl at a real-estate night class and the next week she dropped out. I met another girl at work. It took me two months to get up the nerve to ask her to breakfast. We ate at Denny's. I had the Gram Slam. Everything was excellent except she got transferred before lunch. What on earth can you do when the right women keep disappearing on you?*
—Right into Skinny Air

Dear Skinny Air: Take a cruise. I'm sure you're not at all like my neighbor but let me tell you his philosophy. "They keep escapin'," he says. "Out at the bars I buy them a couple of drinks and then it's like abracadabra seeyalada. I don't know what they do, go in the ladies room and change their hair color and take the rings from their noses and put them in their ears to disguise themselves, I don't know. But they're gone. I run into the parking lot and I don't know if they turn themselves into tiny Alpha Romeos or what, but it's like 'Poof,' disintegration. That's why I go on cruises. They can't get away from me. I just keep trackin' them. Up, down, lido, all around. I don't care. I just keep trailin' them until I wear 'em down and corner them at the end of the night. You know, they've had a half dozen glasses of wine, they're bloated with seventeen courses of that gourmet chow. They're weak, man. Vulnerable. Where they gonna go? Have you ever seen someone turn into an Alpha Romeo while they're surrounded by a black sea and pressed up against the railing on the third level of a cruise ship headed for the Bahamas? Do you understand? I've got 'em on a boat. Do you understand? A ship, a floating vessel . . ." I understand, but then I've been living next door to him for seven and a half years.

Dear Gangster: *I'm a guy who likes guys. What I don't like are bars. Because of all the homophobia it is hard to be open and meet guys in an environment that isn't sexually charged or doesn't survive on the selling of liquor. I don't live in San Francisco, but in a small town ninety miles away that doesn't have the gay culture that San Francisco has. How can I meet guys?*   **—Ready to Fall in Love**

Dear Ready to Fall: I'm a guy who likes girls. I'd be a fool to say I can identify with what you're going through. But you'd be a fool to ignore how difficult love is for all of us. Whether you're a gay living in Petticoat Junction or a straight in Chicago there are no easy passages. I've spent plenty of nights myself in places that survive on liquor in hopes of meeting someone. I've reached out to the wrong hands on several occasions when I knew the only thing it would bring was a few hours of closeness. It seems most of the search for love is built on acts of desperation. I can't talk in miles, or cultures, or environments. I met the first person I truly loved a thousand miles from where I lived, in a drugstore. Four years later she moved a thousand miles away from where we both lived. A day later I was sick with desperation. My only advice, and I'd give you this whether you were gay or straight, is stay desperate. Alive and desperate, I like to say, because in some twisted way it leads to love. I hope, for both our sakes.

Dear Gangster: *My boyfriend has had a tough life. More complicated than I can begin to tell. I really care about him but he seems to have this knack of being able to turn his feelings for me on and off. Right now it's off.* **—Where's the Switch**

Dear Switch Hunter: I have a close friend who did some war time and then eventually a lot of drunk time back home but he's had the same girl sticking by him since high school. His coldness sometimes pains him terribly. I've heard him say, "I love and then I can't love, I love and then I can't love, I love and then I can't love." It's a vicious rhythm that he can't seem to shake. His girl is left never knowing what the distance is at any given time. I asked her how she keeps it going and she told me that she fought with it for a while but then realized all she can do is love him . . . all the time.

Dear Gangster: *Is young love the only true love?*
—You Can Guess if You Want To

Dear If I Want To: To answer this I called my high school sweetheart out of the blue after fifteen years. She weighs like twenty-two hundred pounds. She didn't say so but I could tell by her heavy breathing and the time it took her to switch the phone from one shoulder to the other. After I asked her if her sister was still a tramp I asked if she was happy? "I guess so," she said, which I guess is as good a guess as any. I don't know what I expected her to say? "No, all I think about is you, my love." It upset me to think that the most important person in my life for several years was now a tiny memory. Maybe young love isn't worth that much in the big scheme. If early love was real, could it be dismissed so easily? I tried to keep the remainder of the call cute. She mentioned she had twins. "I never would have done that to you," I told her. Next time it's your turn to call, I insisted, "or maybe one of those picture Christmas cards would do, O.K.? Slap one of the twins for me and don't tell me which one." I hung up and stared into the possibility that there is no such thing as love.

Dear Gangster: *I'm a forty-two-year-old male. I want someone who can easily fit into my life the way it is now. The way it's going to stay.* **—I Know EXACTLY What I Want**

Dear Exactly: Someone to blend into the pattern of your couch, someone who likes the smell of your honeysuckle Renuzits in every freakin' room of the house, someone who will lie on their back during sex and make little gurgling noises just like the filter on your fish tank. You are looking for a person to fit into the Goddamned hole it took you forty-two years to dig for yourself and you're not foolin' around, are you?

Dear Gangster: *Do you think the ruling that permits the registration of an official companion really serves a purpose?* **—Companion Seeking Purpose**

Dear Companion Seeking Purpose: The last time I was in a gay establishment the clientele were splashing the walls with pastel paint and blowing up inflatable beach toys for no apparent reason. Other than perhaps, fun. As I joined in and puffed into a medium-sized Shamu I wondered if all this activity was a way of coping with the times and if sex could have possibly been replaced by . . . fun. My guess is, my guess was wrong and I know nothing about life. If you are asking if I think everyone should be able to write their wills and leave each other their splashes of vibrant color, their inflatable whales and sweet memories of love . . . Yes, yes I do, my friend.

Dear Gangster: *I woke up last weekend and said to myself, "Jesus, it's time to get married."* **—Is That Shallow?**

Dear Is That: As the hand-dug graves of a mass murderer. But nothing to be ashamed of. It's what the majority of humans do. For most of us it is very obvious that the man or woman you marry could have easily been someone else. Someone better. We pluck from a selection as numbered and contained as a jukebox's. When you finally decide IT'S TIME there's a good chance the person you loved a few relationships back when it WASN'T TIME might have been the person you should have spent the rest of your life with. And now that love is lost forever. Isn't this great to think about?

Dear Gangster: *Your answer to "Plain & Simple" really hit me. I fell in love and he said he wasn't ready to commit and he doesn't believe in love. He ended the friendship but I get phone calls from people I don't know and I know it must have something to do with him. I don't understand what he wants. He knows I love only him. What do I do? I can't take it.* **—Moving Soon**

Dear Soon: We grab on to a lot of things in life. Some good for us. Some pretty bad for us. But to grab on to someone who says to your face, "I don't believe in love," is pretty scary. I like it.

Dear Gangster: *I was talking to one of my buddies recently about a girl we had both been going out with. She had always refused to perform oral sex on me but I just found out, to my surprise, she always took care of him. And I went out with her longer than he did. I didn't say anything when he mentioned it but it's been eating at me. I'm getting real self-conscious about it. Is it the way I look? Is it because my car's too small? Is it my freckles?* **—One of the Chosen, Not**

Dear Not: Thanks for the graduation pictures of you two by the way. Now if I had a choice, I mean, if it was one of those things where you'd ask me to choose and I would try to joke it off by saying, "I'd pick the girlfriend," and then you said, "No, damn it, stop the kidding. You have to choose one of these two." If you really pinned me down like that, well, I'd go with your buddy Andrew there in a heartbeat. But who am I to be selecting the high-school boy I'd most like to perform oral sex on? So I've decided we'll print the pictures here next week and have a reader call-in survey. You'll have your answer in a couple of weeks.

Dear Gangster: *I've been seeing these two guys simultaneously and some nights they both call about the same time. I have call waiting so I can click back and forth between the two of them. Back and forth, back and forth. The thing is, I find this to be such a turn on that I don't even want to see them anymore. I just want them to call me.* **—Breathless**

Dear Breathless: I could probably come up with some witty reply referring back to speed dialing but I'm sick of this. I'm not answering any more questions without pictures. I think some of you people are starting to make this stuff up. I don't care if you never want to see those two guys again. I want to. I want graduation pictures of both of them, and one of you and the phone separate and one of you and the phone together and maybe a close-up of call waiting. Has anyone ever really gotten a good shot of call waiting? Somebody'd better. I want pictures. Words are too easy for you people.

I HAVEN'T GOT TIME FOR PEOPLE WHO DON'T FEEL SORRY FOR ME

Dear Gangster: *I seem to have hooked up with Mr. Procrastinator. Every time I talk about marriage he always says he just has one more thing he wants to do before he ties the big knot around his throat.* **—Gettin' the Lasso Out**

Dear Lasso: Many still believe life ends with marriage. I knew these two brothers who kept an extensive list of things they had to do before either one could get married. And they just kept adding to it so they'd never ever get married. One would say, "That's it I'm gonna ask her to marry me," and the other would run for the list and say, "But, but . . . you've never instigated a pi-ano sing-along." Yes, you're right brother, I must get that out of my system and what do we have after that? "You've never been to the Stone Pony. And you've probably seen films of Russians lining up at McDonald's but have you ever actually seen one sink teeth into a Big Mac and have you ever had your own bookie? I mean, ever been able to say to someone, 'Excuse me, I have to call my bookie.'?" No, I'll have to get that out of my system before I can give myself totally to the woman I love. Now, what else was there? "Have you ever worked a parcel of land? You know there are still places in this country where they'll give you a piece of land to work if you agree to grow Pixy Stix or some pre-ordained crop and didn't you say just the other day that you've never had a Personal Pan Pizza, that you've always had to share pizzas?"

Dear Gangster: *I think what I originally loved about this person I'm living with is what I hate about this person now. All the little eccentricities, they seemed so sweet when we were dating, but now the idea that he cuts his sandwiches into nine tiny triangles seems stupid. Especially when I'm in a hurry. And the way he calls for the weather and the time six or seven times a day used to make me laugh. Now it makes me hate the weather and the time of day. And when he put the steer horns on the Honda. Maybe it's just me, or maybe I'll just kill him and then call for the time of death.*

—Not Waiting for an Answer

Dear Not Waiting: You know what you have to do. There's a fine line between loving someone and wanting to slice them up into nine tiny triangles. Why is it that we find eccentricities so endearing until we don't want to anymore? I remember this one girl I was crazy about, before I knew her of course. From a distance she was this flippant girl-woman, kind of a cross between Liz Phair and Faith Daniels. She pranced when she walked and she ducked when people spoke to her as if their voices were going to smack her in the face. She dressed like somebody owed her something and she somehow smiled while forming her mouth into a perfect "O." I was crazy about her.

Then I went to her place. And it was exactly like you would have pictured it if you'd already known she was nuts. Don't get me wrong, I like nutty. I like to take nutty out to dinner. I like to walk nutty forty yards out on a seaside dock while licking sherbet cones. I like to exchange dreams with nutty. I like to have oral sex with nutty on the third date but I also like to sit down.

Not a chair in the place. I had to struggle to find something to lean on. She had all these partition things, I forget what they call them. The kind of thing Kitty on Gunsmoke would change behind. Picture about ten of those all jumbled up in a two-hundred-square-foot apartment. I was there for four minutes and lost her five times. Even when I could hear her I couldn't find her. I finally looked up as if I might see a shadow on the ceiling and saw, attached to her A/C vents, multicolored streamers like you see on new bicycles. They were beautiful.

Beautiful that is compared to the Troll dolls that seemed to have had their heads shaved. "I'm a Troll barber now," she giggled. That's kind of the way it was. One second I'd spot something off-putting but then it would be counteracted by something like the High Plains Drifter movie poster taped to her fridge, which I really dug. She also had several bars of soap by her kitchen sink that had plastic feet, hands, and noses. Mr. Potato Head paraphernalia? These are just for show, I suppose? "No, no," she said. "I use them all the time. I just put the body parts back on when I'm done. The bars get smaller but the ears always stay the same size."

I was getting less crazy about her by the minute. But she kept grabbing me with her style. When I asked why she had huge holes in the middle of all the window shades, she said, "So the moon can see in every window. Don't want to keep the moon out." I headed into the bathroom, mainly to sit down, but I was surrounded by kitty-litter boxes. I couldn't even sit on the toilet without having to stick my feet in kitty litter. I was sitting there levitating them, kind of a lavatorial yoga move, when she called in, "You can use the kitty-litter shoes if you have to go to the bathroom. One size fits all." She had special kitty-litter shoes so that you could rest your feet amongst the litter while using the toilet. I couldn't believe it. Even after I had them on I couldn't believe it. Finally I believed it.

You can only be so crazy about someone who drives you nuts. It took me a half hour to find the door but at least she couldn't see me leaving. It wasn't until I got home in my own kitchen and dropped a spatula that I realized I was still wearing kitty-litter shoes. In my own kitchen! In the room where I boil my noodles, where I make my most important phone calls, where I see myself in my china, where I bend over to pick up a spatula and come face to face with the kitty shoes of a woman who flipped my heart with her strangeness. I still think of her, wish her the best, and occasionally curse myself for not being able to accept the only woman I've ever known that the moon takes a good hard look at every night.

Dear Gangster: *I have this one guy who calls me up to go out but usually the first two hours of our date he expects me to go around with him while he does all these stupid errands. How do I get him to only pick me up for the good stuff: the dinner, the show, the peck on the cheek?* **—No Errand Girl**

Dear No Errand: I hate that. And some people turn it into these errand marathons. A friend of mine was telling me that he got stuck (he begged her) tagging along with this one woman for an entire day. "And at every stop, after she was helped, the clerk would turn to me and say, 'Can I help you?' Florist. 'Can I help you?' Post Office. 'Can I help you?' Photo place. 'Can I help you?' Couldn't they tell I was with her, for God's sake? What did they think, she was too beautiful (she is) to be seen with me? Couldn't they see I was at her side, not behind her? Anyway, I just kept saying, 'No, I'm with her. No, I'm with her. No, I'm with her.' I must have said, 'No, I'm with her,' thirteen times in one day. What a schlep. 'No, I'm with her." I finally cracked at the dry cleaners and said, 'Yes sir, you can help me,' and took off my shirt and pants and handed them over.

"Now, she won't let me follow her around anymore."

Dear Gangster: *It's my girlfriend's hair. It's so large and she sprays so much stuff on it that it's become like a protective shield around her. I can't stand to even touch it. She says everybody at the office gets up at 5:30 in the morning to build hair like this. But what is this?*
                                             —Can't Touch This

Dear This: And it looks good, doesn't it? You just want to run your fingers through it, bury your nose in there and suck up the aroma of each strand, swim with broad strokes through all the loops and curls, you wanna leap into it like a child wants to jump into a pile of leaves. DON'T DO IT. What you've been doing so far is exactly right. Stand back and admire. Steer clear. I've heard that many women spritz and spritz until even the split ends are hard enough to cut glass. Check her bathroom mirror for scratches. I also know this poses a sex problem and I don't know what to tell you. Maybe try doing something like the Muslims do and just have sex through a hole in a sheet or through a hole in a public bathroom stall like they do in some neighborhoods. It could be exciting. Just don't say I didn't warn you. I had one friend who wouldn't listen until somebody got hurt. His lady had her hair all rolled up at the top. "It was a two-and-a-half-hour job," he told me. During sex he was always doing strange maneuvers to avoid it. "She loved it," he said. "She called me the erotic acrobat." Anyway, one afternoon in the clenches he came right down on top of it. "It was like barbed wire, seventeen stitches across my chin," he said. "But let me tell ya, in the emergency room, everyone was complimenting her hair. It was perfect."

Dear Gangster: *I live for my social life and so does my boyfriend. The problem is I'm tired of him but he's extremely popular and I don't think I'd get invited to half as many parties without him. Do I just keep hanging on?*　　　　　　　　　**—Party Girl**

Dear PG: I figured this out once for a friend of mine who trained sea lions and seals at an aquarium. You might think someone like that would not be into heavy partying but like she used to say, "What am I supposed to be into, splashing?" Anyway, she was involved with a grand prix driver. Somebody gets a new patch on their jacket and these guys are poppin' a cork on a yacht somewhere. Well, at some point he began to repulse her but she was so wired into "the scene" she couldn't let go. To put her dilemma into perspective I put it all on paper comparing the honest six to eight minutes of actual sexual encounters to the hours of late night partying that was "fabulously fulfilling" four to five times a week. We then calculated the wee bit of time she actually spent alone with him, like the few seconds it would take to watch him try on his clothes between parties and say, "You look like a shrimp cocktail salesman in those loafers." Then we factored in the good—that he was out of town forty-eight days of the year trying to woo sponsors. And the bad—the burnout and the Mary Tyler Moore woodgrain complexion she'd pick up between the yachts and the sea lion matinees. Anyway, on a yearly basis we figured if she left him she'd be giving up over forty-four thousand hours of glorious partying because of the mere forty-four minutes she'd had to spend with a jerk. No contest.

Dear Gangster: *I am a twenty-five-year-old brunette bombshell. I'm a cross between Demi Moore and Jasmine Guy. I have brains, a career (sales rep and artist), and good looks. I'm honest when it comes to relationships and I don't do drugs, smoke or drink. I am physically fit and someday (very soon I hope) I'll make a great wife and mother. Now you're probably wondering what kind of problem I could possibly have. I can't find a decent man who wants the same things I do. The only men I seem to attract are either in San Quentin or on their way. Where are all the decent "old fashioned guys?" Help!*

—**Hating the Single Life in San Jose**

Dear Single in Jose: Is the question, "Why aren't old fashioned guys attracted to a Jasmine Guy/Demi Moore type that calls herself a bombshell?" What would this old fashioned guy be? A cross between Ken Berry and Tommy Lasorda? Would he call himself "strapping?" And what do you mean by "old fashioned" anyway? Someone who bites a bullet when they get their appendix taken out? Someone who dreams of having a stroke while shoveling snow? Someone who practices the rhythm method? Did I tell you I once did a survey at San Quentin and one of the questions was "Describe your ideal mate." The most common reply was "A cross between Jasmine Guy and Demi Moore that lives nearby." If I were you I'd stop your whining and do something different with your hair.

Dear Gangster: *I get upset easily and my boyfriend doesn't understand. He thinks I'm irrational. He says, "You don't have to get upset if you don't want to." How can I make him understand?*

—**Upset**

Dear Upset: He doesn't have to understand if he doesn't want to.

Dear Gangster: *Since I broke up with the only woman I ever loved I'm nothing. Nobody. I have no shape or form.*

—**I'm Just . . . Just**

Dear Just: If you jumped in a pool would there be a splash? If you wrapped yourself in aluminum foil would you attract the sun's attention? I love when love leaves you with these questions of being. When you eat do your shoes fill up with food? If you stand in front of an x-ray machine does your heart take the shape of a chocolate bunny? Is it hollow? Does it look like its ears were just bitten off by a deceitful angel? Do people point at you across the room and shout, "There he was!"

Dear Gangster: *I don't know if I'm a bad person or just opportunistic. This girl, who I admit I'd never have a chance with in a normal situation, has been very ill lately and all I can think is—now's my chance, now's my chance.*

—**Ready to Move in for the Kill**

Dear For the Kill: I get it, you're Mr. Sympathetic while all the other boys are staying away. And then when she's better—when the color comes back, the muscles start to firm up—and she's ready to go dancing, you'll be the one she thinks of first. Not a bad concept. I had an associate who pulled this with a woman who was recovering from surgery. While all the usual suspects were letting her recover in peace he was knocking on her apartment door with bags of groceries, doing wash, changing sheets, and bringing over children's story books to read at her bedside. What a cute touch, what woman wouldn't melt from the kiddy books? By the time she was better she was crazy about him but as far as he was concerned it was over. "It went through all the usual steps of a relationship," he said. "We talked intimately, we laughed at the silliest things, we held hands, we fought over what talk shows to watch, I started to dwell on how she chewed her food, and the whole thing probably peaked for me when I got a glimpse of her naked as her bathrobe got caught on the bathroom door right after I'd read her the Berenstain Bears' *Inside, Outside, Upside Down*, but it was downhill from there. We were in love, then we got to know each other, then we weren't. The usual."

Dear Gangster: *Hey, it's too late for me but I want to tell everybody that they should ask a lot about people while they're still alive. I had this guy coming on to me for months but I always blew him off. Well, he died about ten days ago and everybody was talking about him and if half these stories are true then he was a really neat guy. I should have jumped on him while I had the chance.*

—**Oh Well, Too Late**

Dear Oh Well: I had a girl blaming me a few months back for not clueing her in on a friend of mine. "I was in the same room with this guy and you never told me any of this," she said while reading the obituary at my kitchen table. He was semi-well known so the paper went into quite a bit of detail. "He raised llamas. I love llamas," she said.

Everybody loves llamas I told her. I think that's why he had them. To pick up chicks. "He did not," she said. "I was in the same room with him once and I know he's not that type."

"Well, you're the authority," I said.

"He went to Juilliard," she yelped. "How come he didn't say anything? Most guys, that would be the first thing out of their mouths."

"It was fifteen years ago," I said.

"Still," she said.

"Listen," I said. "Most people are very interesting when you list the highlights in a few paragraphs. Even I'd be . . .

"Yeah, right," she said. "God, he was a SEAL."

"Let me see that," I said ripping it out of her hands. "Now, that's a lie. He wasn't no SEAL. Everybody's claiming they were a SEAL now. How the hell'd he get that in . . ."

"Look, it's closed coffin. He was very cool wasn't he?" she said. "I never did understand why people leave the lid up. Most of us won't even come to the door in our bathrobes 'cause our hair might not look just right and then in the end we put a notice in the paper for everyone to come see us dead. Does that make sense to you?"

While I was taking a moment to think about it she pulled the paper to her bosom and whispered, "I'm in love."

Dear Gangster: *It's time for the blood test and I'm getting a little fidgety. Like I'm a shy little boy, which I am. I used to hear clinics on the radio saying, "Come on down! It's AIDS awareness day. Come and get a free test." But I haven't heard that in a while. Besides, I'd rather just go to my own doctor, but what do I say on the phone?*

—Hello I'd Like a . . .

Dear Hello: Making an appointment for a blood test is to the '90s what asking the druggist for a box of condoms was to the '50s. You call the doctor. You say hello to the receptionist. What's your name? Hillary, I have an aunt named Hillary. She has a dog named Jackson. Oh, you have a cat. What are the hours at the shop now? Does Dr. Shapiro still only work mornings on Thursday? I remember the last time I was in for the hiccups. You might remember me. I was hiccuping. Do you still take Blue Cross Blue

Shield? Last time I filled out that form and I always check all the no's. I do it automatically because I've never had anything. I'm like on "automatic no" when I fill out those things. No hepatitis. No tuberculosis. No, No, No. I'm in perfect health, you know. Never felt better.

"Sir, this is just the doctor's answering service. If you want a blood test you'll have to call back in an hour."

Dear Gangster: *I'm losing a bit of my perception when it comes to being able to tell whether someone is trying to take advantage of me or win my heart.*
> **—Not That Either One Wouldn't Do at This Point**

Dear At This Point: If we can fool someone into falling in love with us then we are certainly taking advantage of that person. I think any one of us would agree with that, especially at this point.

Dear Gangster: *Even if you are content with your mate is there always a better love out there somewhere?*
> **—Just Wondering Again**

Dear Just Wondering: There's such a big difference between being OUT there and being IN there. When you're IN there you always assume there is something better OUT there but when you're OUT there never is. Am I making sense? I gotta start gettin' OUT more.

Dear Gangster: *My boyfriend and I have been through some rough times lately but I really want things to work out. I know this is the guy for me. Last night he said the way things are going it'll be a miracle if we're together a year from now. I kind of agree because*

it doesn't seem like either one of us is ever going to change. So, do I just keep my fingers crossed and my eyes out for shooting stars?
—**Counting on a Miracle**

Dear Counting: Miracles. I once had this can of Barbasol menthol shaving cream that seemed to run dry every morning I used it, but then the next day I was able to squeeze out just enough for one more shave. This went on for years. At first I thought it was the menthol, but it wasn't. It was a miracle. I still have the can but don't use it on a daily basis anymore. There's something about starting every day off with a miracle that makes me uneasy. Oh, and did I tell you I once saw a baby roll off the hood of a car and float down to the pavement? What else? There was the time I was at Disney's Epcot Center in Orlando, Florida where they have exhibits from several countries and I was somehow able to say, in eight different languages, including Moroccan, "And how much are your handbags?" It just came out. I've got the pocketbooks to prove it. The only reason I'm telling you this is to let you know I do believe in miracles. I don't, however, believe you can predict them or count on them when it comes to love. Parting seas and magic shaving cans are one thing. Love is another.

And I think it might have been on MTV that I saw that floating baby.

Dear Gangster: *I'm in love. You have won my heart. Please write a little bit about yourself in your next column.*
—**Under Your Spell**

Dear Under: I thought that all I did was write about myself. But if you're not getting enough I'll let a few things slip now and then and you can write periodically and we'll keep adding.

Trickle down effect. First thing you should know is I have this Swedish Mentality Syndrome. I don't know why the Swedes get credit for this but it means you will do almost anything to avoid a confrontation with another human being. So, naturally, people trample all over me. I like to fly kites and although I've always been a law abiding citizen I believe I will be shot down by a police officer, probably on a Thursday. In my mind I've been married about seventeen times. In reality, I talked to a woman once. Another woman, twice. I raise Great Danes and my only friend is a bridge tender near my house. I walk up there periodically and we talk about things like how black and white everything always looks on his little TV and he'll sometimes say aloud, "Here comes a big one," and I sometimes repeat what he says. It's good therapy. My favorite singers are Tony Bennett and Warren Zevon. I have this dream that someday I will do something so outstanding it will culminate with four triple back flips and a tearful hug from Bela Karolyi. My biggest fear is that after reading this you will be even more entranced by my existence. I'm crazy about you too.

Dear Gangster: *My gal embarrasses so easily. She's so cautious because she thinks someone might see her make a fool of herself. How do I loosen her up? What's wrong with making a fool of yourself?*

—**A Fool**

Dear Fool: That's easy for you to say. But there's something inbred in a lot of us that makes us forever self-conscious and it's hard to dismiss those gut feelings on a whim. There may be no valid reason to care, but how do you stop yourself? An associate of mine's first reaction whenever he messes up is to look around and see if anyone noticed. That's all he cares about. I'm sure if he accidentally tumbled into a wood shredder and was mutilated into a thousand fragments his upper and lower lip would somehow struggle to find each other and utter those final words, "Did anybody see me do that?"

Dear Gangster: *How close do you have to be to someone before you can spill your guts? I finally felt like I could tell this girl everything and just when I was in the middle of an emotional outpouring she put her hands up like she was going to cradle me but instead shouted, "Whoa, we're not that close." What does it take these days? How much time do you have to spend with someone? How much money do you have to spend on them before there's a real bond? How many times do you have to have sex with someone before you can honestly talk to them, ten, twenty?* **—Tell Me When**

Dear Tell Me: Forty-two to be exact.

Dear Gangster: *Why is it some guys think they can step all over you and you're still going to be their little puppy dog? Then when you finally say enough is enough they just say O.K., and kind of step around you and move on. What's going on in these guys' heads?*

—Little Puppy Dog

Dear Dog: I played softball with this one couple and knew them both about equally until the guy started really treating the girl like garbage. It became nauseating because it seemed like she was always trying to tip-toe around him and be sweet but he'd turn on her anyway. I figured I was only seeing one side of it but I met the guy alone recently and he said proudly, "No, it was all me." And he told me how he finally kicked her out of his place because she didn't get the message. What message, I wondered. What was going on in his head? "I don't really know either," he said offhandedly. "She's not the first one I had to get rid of. And you know, to tell you the truth, I think I hurt her for the same reason I hurt the others. She just got in the path of my way of thinking." I made him repeat that last line because I found it frighteningly profound and I wondered if he'd heard himself the first time.

He said, "I said, 'She just got in the path of my way of thinking.' What's the matter, didn't you hear me the first time?"

Dear Gangster: *I've just been through a bad relationship. In fact, it's the second one in a row. I can live with it though. My real problem is my closest friends. They all seem to be involved in perfect relationships and can't help consoling me on the fact that I can't seem to make anything work. They all feel soooo sorry for me.*

—Sorry Seems to Be the Hardest Word

Dear Sorry: You can never have too many people around who feel sorry for you. I keep adding new ones all the time. I have one of those phones that you can program to speed dial your nine most important numbers and I have it set up with only people who will automatically feel sorry for me. It's in order too. If I want someone who will just feel a little sorry for me I dial one and so on. For a big crisis I hit the nine where I know the person on the other end will, having sensed my pain, pick up sobbing and run to the house to give me a sponge bath and cradle me till daybreak. Maybe I'm not the right person to help you with this problem because, myself, I haven't got time for people who don't feel sorry for me.

YOUR REAL PROBLEM IS THE WRATH OF GOD

Dear Gangster: *I got set up with this guy for a blind date and everything was fun and fast the night we went out, but when we went to brunch the next morning, in broad daylight, I realized how much he looked like a guy I can't stand. Now I can't get it out of my head and I'm like taking it out on this poor guy. What should I do?*

—Double the Hate

Dear Double: Run like hell. Don't let it go any further. My accountant is mixed up in a situation like this and it's more than ugly. It involves Kurt Loder. He's a dead ringer. When he and his wife got married she didn't even know who Kurt was, but later she got so revolted by those cross-legged namby-pamby pseudo voodoo question and answer sessions on MTV she pulled the plug on the marriage. "While he was making love to me I could hear that voice," she said. "It was saying something to Tom Petty about the honor involved with being a Wilbury and I just screamed. 'That's it. It's over.'" Now, the beautiful part about this is the guy doesn't know the real reason she demanded a divorce. She just told him some garbage about how she had to be alone. This is where I come in. She wants me to break the truth. The Kurt statute is up, I guess. He's out of town but I've been calling his house everyday. I wanna say it so bad, "You lost the best thing you ever had because of Kurt Loder." Even the most sensible chap could lose it under those circumstances. Man, Kurt better be watching the shadows when my accountant gets back in town.

Dear Gangster: *With my last girlfriend I was always rifling through her purse or going in her medicine cabinet and pretty much living on the premise that what was hers was mine. We'd been together for years and everything was fine. But with my new girl I guess I jumped the gun a little bit. After only six weeks she's refusing to see me because I took a pack of pocket-size tissues out of her bathroom closet without asking. She wouldn't even have known except they're scented and she smelt them in my car. I keep telling her it was only tissues, pocket-size even, but she says that's not the point. Is there any chance of turning this around?* **—It Takes a Thief**

Dear Thief: I remember the Lifesavers as if it were yesterday. I was sitting at her desk. She said, "Go ahead, honey, sit at my desk. I'll be out all afternoon." I said, "O.K., baby." We'd been honey and baby for about four days at this point. I was going for a pen when I saw them in the drawer and it was so innocent. It was like a hand turned to you, gave you a glimpse of the rainbow pack, and said, in that Löwenbräu friends-for-eternity tone, "Life-saver?"

Yes. Yes, don't mind if I do. And do you care if I dig three deep for the orange?

I can't even blame it on the digging because as soon as I touched the roll the wrapper went to pieces. Like it'd been mummified for centuries and suddenly come in contact with oxygen. I knew I was in trouble. I didn't know this girl that well. I shouldn't have been a taker yet. And when I saw nothing but the foil, the Lifesaver jacket completely disintegrated, the nakedness of the situation crippled me. It was so obvious that the roll had been tampered with. I shut the drawer and opened it real quick to view how noticeable it would be at first glance and I was practically blinded. The silver wrap was almost like a mirror when the light hit it. You'd have to shield your eyes to find anything in the desk except the Lifesavers. What if I just took them and threw them out or placed the small silver cylinder in my sock and made a run for it? Better gone and possibly forgotten than blinding and obviously tampered with by the last person who sat at my desk and slept in my bed.

I was thinking like a criminal when I popped the little orange doughnut. It was old. It was stinkin' mildewy old. I could hear it now, "He not only steals, Becky, he steals that which is old and rotten."

I put 'em in my sock.

Needless to say we never made it to the fifth day. "Hi, baby," I said when she got back. "Hi, h . . . , what the heck happened to my Lifesavers?" she said.

"Oh, they were old. I threw them out," I said.

"They weren't old. I just bought them downstairs yesterday. How could you tell anyway? You didn't take one did you?"

"No, no, they stunk. Smelled them as soon as I opened the drawer," I said.

"Candy doesn't stink when it goes bad."

"Of course it does. Everything stinks when it goes bad." I could sense I was starting to stink so I changed my tune. I decided to go with a series of three-word-truths. "I took one. They were bad. Threw them out."

"If they were bad I would have returned them. Why were you touching them anyway? What the hell gives you the right to . . ."

"To take a Lifesaver? To suck on a simple Lifesaver after everything we've had and shared together?"

"I've only known you for four days, I don't need someone taking things from me the first chance they get. I don't nee . . ."

"Like I need someone who would actually return a pack of stale Lifesavers. Like I need to be involved with the nickel and dimin' Lifesaver returnin' type."

"Just get away from me. No, give me my candies back first. Where are they? I know you didn't eat them all. I know you didn't throw them out."

Jesus, she really could know a person pretty well after only four days.

"You wanna see my tongue?" I lashed out. "You want to see if it's every color of the rainbow?"

"Just get away from me!"

"Yeah, why don't I just get in and out of your life in less than a week."

I know you're out there, Sara. They were in my sock the whole time, you miser of all that's good and sweet and colorful in this world. You never would have found them. You never would have tasted how old and mildewy and decrepit they had become after only one day in your possession. Imagine how I felt after four days.

Dear Gangster: *Ever since I was a little girl I've had this thing about not being able to unpack. I just can't stand the "settled in"* *feeling that I experience if I'm not packed and ready to go. My partner is a nester and perceives my inability to unpack as being messy. Remember the movie where Jack Nicholson was in Washington state and got into the truck and just rode away? The trucker asked him if he had a jacket and all he could think of was, if he had always kept his jacket and wallet packed he wouldn't have to be getting into a cold truck heading north without a jacket or lunch money.*

  —You Never Know When You Might Have to Leave in a Hurry

Dear You Never Know: I do remember when Nicholson got in the truck and I remember when Jennifer got into the MR2 and I remember Nan got into a Range Rover and I can still see Karin getting into that old convertible, her red hair flying behind her like a baron's scarf. And I remember Bonnie's last words being, "I know we could talk more and maybe you could change my mind but the cab's here. We're not the only ones waiting now." And I remember Karol leaving in my car and me having to fly to Houston to get it back. And I wish you wouldn't have reminded me of all these people.

Dear Gangster: *You're sweet but you're sick too. Who raised you?*   **—Tired of Trying to Figure You Out**

Dear Tired: An angel who told me she only took the job so she could fly. And I miss her dearly.

Dear Gangster: *Happy New Year!*   **—Cindi**

Dear Cindi: Happy New Year!

Dear Gangster: *I had to write you. I can't take it any longer. As I sit downtown at JJ's, not only listening to the blues but car-*

rying a heavy case of my own, I think my gal of two months wants to leave me. She is dancing with some big guy and she knows it drives me mad. I can't take it anymore and I love her. I think she just does it to bother me. I would be better for her and her two children than any guy she dances with. What should I do? —**Arthur Murray I'm Not**

Dear I'm Not: Thanks for writing this on the back of JJ's menu by the way. That cajun skinless chicken breast sounds good about now. Ohh, they got those catfish tidbits for an appetizer and nachos grande. What is it with nachos now? For some reason I don't want anything to do with them anymore. I guess they kinda peaked in movie theaters and then some of the theaters started running little concession commercials before the feature, didn't they? They'd flash a slide of nachos but it was never a real professional shot. The lighting would be too bright and nachos aren't something you want to zoom in on with a spotlight and take a real good hard moltened look at. But I'm sure at JJ's they'd say, "Wait a second, these ain't no movie theater nachos," and the people at the next table over would verify it, "And you've got to have their salsa. It's the best." But I don't think I could be swayed to the nachos unless it was to take my mind off the big man in town dancing with my woman and even then . . . bread pudding with whiskey sauce? That sounds good. But where do you go from there. "Can I get you anything else?" "Ahh, the bread pudding with whiskey sauce." But then what? "Check please?" Can you eat something like that and then go home and watch *Nightline*? Do you take a long drive or make a short distance call to someone who will recognize your voice immediately? Do you close your eyes and listen to the music or make small talk with the couple at the next table—the salsa experts? Or do you maybe order one more bread pudding with whiskey sauce, lick your spoon, get up and walk across a smothering dance floor, step in

front of a big man, look into the dark eyes of the woman you love
and say, "Baby, will ya teach me how to dance?"

Dear Gangster: *My boyfriend makes the biggest deal about
the boots I wear. He says I wear them way too much and they make me
look "butch," whatever that means. At first I thought he was kidding
but he never lets up. I told him he has to like me for who I am. These
boots are me. And I'm not foolin', you'd have to see them, but they're
me, definitely me. He says, "You didn't have them when I met you.
They're not the you you made me think you were," or something like
that. I'm me. I tell him, but he just keeps gnawing away at it. Should I
give in?*   **—Boots II Men**

Dear Boots: I wish people would send me some more
menus. Sometimes it only takes one little thing to reveal a major
flaw in one's character. I was deeply in love with this woman
once. I would do anything for her. I would even go to the drugstore for her. One morning she called me and her throat was so
sore she could barely talk. "Could you pick me up some
lozenges?" Of course I could, and I wrote down the kind she
wanted. I think they were called Marions. Anyway, when I got to
the checkout there was a bit of a line and while fumbling with the
box I noticed the fine print: Excellent for speaking engagements.
They were like "hahmm" drops. This couldn't be what she
wanted, I thought, so I called her. "Are you sure you want these
particular lozenges because . . . " "Don't they say they're good for
public speaking on the back?" She knew, she knew all along. I
was stunned. "Yes but no," I said. "No, what?" she rasped. "No," I
said. And that was it. No, I cannot spend anymore time with you.
No, I cannot love you anymore. No, I am not buying the
lozenges. Sometimes it's so clear that you've made a mistake. People can trick you and con you and toss their hair in a certain way

during intercourse to keep you rapt but sooner or later they slip up—maybe it's a pair of thick-soled boots or a skinny lozenge made for "speaking engagement people," but all of the men and women I've ever known eventually give themselves away. It's our culture, you know, that causes such deception in the first place. Someday America is going to come out of hiding and I'm gonna fall in love with someone I actually know.

Dear Gangster: *Does it only make it harder to start a new relationship if you look like a famous person? I sort of look like somebody, at least that's what a lot of people tell me. And I often wonder if certain people are just asking me out because of some fantasy. How can I tell?*
—Marie Osmond

Dear Marie: Oh, what I'd like to do to . . . talk about fantasies. My cousin, the ophthalmologist, who has absolutely no sense, approached a woman at my neighbors' party with the words, "You know, you look just like the lady on the Massengill boxes." She just looked at him like she should have under the circumstances but he kept going. "No, really, you do. I never forget a face."

At that point I kind of stepped forward to cut him off but then he said the words, "I'll show you," and I immediately backed off. I wanted to see this.

Sure enough he ran off toward the bathroom, in the people's bedroom no less, but he got nabbed by the hostess. "What are you doing, put that back," I heard my neighbor yelling. "What are you even doing in this bathroom? Everyone's supposed to use the one in the hallway."

"I've been using this one all afternoon," he yelled right back. "Look, there's a couple of my empty beer cans."

I supposed she looked 'cause then she started cursing and the next thing I heard was her yelling, "Stop!" and then I saw my cousin come into view down the hallway, douche in hand, with my neighbor's husband now in pursuit. This was all very amusing until I heard someone ask who the hell that guy was and someone else announce it was my cousin, the ophthalmologist. That's when I decided to slip out the front door. The last thing I saw was the husband ripping at my cousin's shirt just as he was holding the Massengill box up to the woman's face and yelling, "Look everybody."

The resemblance was uncanny.

Dear Gangster: *I think I'm caring about too many people.*
                                            —Who Cares, I Care

Dear Who Cares: "Half dozen." That's what my friend, Albert, tells me. "Never care about more than a half dozen people at one time. You add one you gotta take one off. And if you donate to like UNICEF or something, showing that you care about everyone in the whole universe, give yourself one for that. That way you only have to care about five real people who have needs and telephones and stuff while 4.2% of your paycheck takes care of the rest." Try it. I've found it works. There's several ways to do the math on it though. By the way, we're thinking about doing an infomercial on this. Stay in touch.

Dear Gangster: *I'm a damn acrobat in bed and I can keep doing it over and over again. I never quit. Never. I used to be so popular with the ladies but lately I'm more like just a plain ol' bat than an acrobat, just hanging upside down in the attic all alone.*
                                —What's Happened to My Sex Appeal?

Dear What's Happened: A woman I was speaking to the other day, very confidentially by the way (I love when people tell me things in confidence), told me that she stopped dating this one guy for the very reasons you describe. As you can understand with AIDS and all, she said, you have to use condoms between sex acts and keep changing them and whatnot. "Well, I'll tell you, he was a great lover. Fantastic. But afterwards I couldn't even get up in the dark without stepping on one or have one drop off the ceiling into my hair. They were all over the place, like sperm mines. You know, we'd be doin' it then snap one off and it would go flying and then on with another. They're like pasta—when they're done they stick to the wall. And everything else. After a while I was picking them off the dog like they were ticks. I was at aerobics class one morning and I was feeling good, very springy like. You guessed it, one stuck to the bottom of each shoe. Air Trojans. No more, I'm telling ya! Once, twice, and I'm a very satisfied woman now."

Dear Gangster: *I've been so sensitive lately. It feels good because I seem to be more caring and unselfish but I just get so emotional about everything. My friends think I'm about to crack. Is something going around or should I be worried?"*   **—It Feels Good**

Dear It Feels: You're about the ninth person, including myself, who has brought this to my attention. I've been swearing that Clinton's brother's soul jumped into me at some point during the final minutes of the convention. I've just been weeping uncontrollably at the tiniest sign of common courtesy. Things like somebody waving me through a stop sign have been crippling me. My lips start quivering, tears are flowing, I'm devastated by the least bit of generosity from my fellow man. The other day someone offered to lick a stamp for me and I went to pieces. I'm emotionally spent. By the time anything of real substance happens in my life I will be completely drained of anything approaching sensitivity. I think the process is that you go from having your own soul to having Clinton's brother's soul to having no soul. If you think you feel good now wait until you get to the last phase and become cold, hard, and unfeeling. I can't wait.

Dear Gangster: *What is it when someone gets the lock on you and you can't even figure out why? You can't think of anything that keeps you coming back but you keep coming back.* **—Locked In**

Dear Locked: I was visiting this acquaintance of mine the other day because he always has Cheez-its. I never buy Cheez-its myself and rarely run across them so I've turned them into kind of a delicacy. Sometimes someone will put out a bowl of some generic cheese cracker but the real Cheez-it, never. And this guy always puts out a fresh bowl. At first I thought he had the same bowl sitting out from a long lost party or something but no, they're fresh. He says he puts 'em out 'cause he knows I'm coming.

Imagine that, someone putting out a fresh bowl of Cheez-its 'cause they know you're coming. I think I might have to upgrade him from an acquaintance to a friend. Anyway, on my last visit, he was pacing up and down, up and down. "She does nothin' for me," he's yelling. "A absolutely nothin'. Not physically, not emotionally, not spiritually. Nothin'. Nothin'. And then he stops, goes pale, looks at me like he's scared to death and says, "God, I hope she calls back."

Dear Gangster: *My fiancé and I were in a restaurant when a fire broke out. It was nothing real serious and no one got hurt, well, not physically anyway. What happened was he was in the men's room* *when they started yelling for everyone to get out. He pushed his way to the dining room to see if I was still there. When he didn't see me he figured I got out safely and walked out the front of the building. In the meantime, we had kind of missed each other because I headed back toward the restrooms. When a gentlemen there told me he'd gotten everyone out of the bathrooms I turned around and went out the front. Well, you should have seen my fiancé's face when he saw me walk out. He went nuts and started blabbing, "How could I have left you inside?" He couldn't handle that he got out first. He was so embarrassed. Since that night nothing's been the same. He says he has to rethink everything. Please, tell him this is stupid.*

—So He Wanted to Save His Own Hide, Big Deal

Dear Big Deal: I don't want to make him feel better or anything but let me tell you about my sister's boyfriend. No, let her tell you.

"My foot slipped off the brake and we were headed for this fence and my shoe was caught and I couldn't get untangled with the gas pedal. We were only going about fifteen miles an hour but still, it was scary, and I'm trying to swerve and I'm doing like all I can when suddenly Mark's head is between me and the steering wheel. Can you guess what he was doing? He was throwing himself in front of my air bag, the son of a bitch. He denied it. Said he was trying to protect me. Right. I wouldn't even have hit the fence if he hadn't blocked my view with his fat head. The impact was nothing, the air bag never even popped out, but I knew right away what he tried to pull to save his freckle-ridden hide and I grabbed his head and started banging it on the steering column and he's screamin' and the horn is going off. It was like Toot— Ahh!, Toot—Ahhhh! God, throwing yourself in front of a loved one's air bag. Can you think of anything worse?"

They're getting married in June.

Dear Gangster: *I've been over this a million times with my girlfriend but maybe if she hears it from you she'll understand. She says she understands you. I'm just the opposite. I think I understand something and then I read you and I don't understand anything. But I think that's your fault, not mine. Now, could you please tell her that just because one person doesn't want to commit to another person it does not mean that person doesn't love that other person.*

—Pure and Simple

Dear P & S: No, it means that person doesn't want to love the other person. Pure and Simple.

Dear Gangster: *This girl from out of state just moved into my building and I helped her get settled and transfer her car registration and showed her how the south elevator is faster than the north and where the maintenance people keep a hose in case she wants to wash her car and a lot of other things and now that she's all settled in and I'm just about to make some more intimate moves on her I get this interesting note thanking me for everything. It says stuff like, "it sure was great to run into someone like you in a new place like this. I sure appreciated all your help and want to thank you so much. Thanks again, Marti." What am I to make of this? Am I right in assuming she left off what she really wanted to say after the "thank you so much?" Like, and please don't come around later with a rented movie and think we're gonna snuggle on the couch and watch it or don't think you're gonna get to touch me now just because you showed me where a garden hose was. Tell me it's just me. I'm always reading too much into everything.*

—Just a Little Paranoid

Dear And Rightly So: You've been dismissed. I'm surprised she didn't end it with a "good riddance" or "I'll give you a call when I need a ride home from getting my wisdom teeth taken out" or "maybe I'll let you watch my cat while I go visit my boyfriend in Tahoe every other weekend" or my favorite, "thanks honey, you remind me so much of my big sister."

Dear Gangster: *I've got this very obvious twitch under my left eye that women I approach are starting to mention after only speaking with me for a few minutes. Now it's all I think about. I'm starting to burrow. Haven't been out in weeks.* **—Ticked Off**

Dear Ticked: What is it with people? I have the same exact problem and it's always, "Hey, your eye is twitching, right there. Did you know your eye is going into convulsions? You've got a twitch, you're twitching, you're twitching."

"I know, I know," I tell them. "It's a permanent affliction. If my left arm were gone would you keep telling me, 'Hey, your left arm is missing?'"

"It's doing it again," they say. They don't understand.

What you have to do, my friend, is what I did. Get a patch. Not a cheap Halloween pirate job. A professional eye patch. You can pick them up at any pharmacy. The one I've got is like the Schwinn of eye patches and it only cost $7. The response has been phenomenal. "Everybody is wearing them on the soaps now," one lady friend told me. Some kids at the mall said it was "coo-oo-ol." And what do you think the first thing a woman would say when she walked into a crowded room you're in?

"Hey, who's the guy in the eye patch?" It's very coo-oo-ol.

Dear Gangster: *How 'bout some fashion advice for both men and women for that first date?*
—Looking for Something New

Dear Looking: Eye patches.

Dear Gangster: *A bunch of us were talking in the office about whether size does count. Last time this came up everyone kind of agreed that it didn't really matter but now a lot of us are thinking maybe that it's all that matters. What do you say?* **—Sizing Up**

Dear Sizing Up: I don't know if this topic came up for the same reason it did with me but I was discussing this with some brothers just the other day. And the reason we were thinking size does matter now is because of some of the recent incidents where women decide to, how should we put this, "dismember" a fellow while he's sleeping. Because, the thing is, when they've got to send someone back to find it SIZE MEANS EVERYTHING. "Who do they send anyway?" somebody said. "Does someone at the hospital have that job, retrieving limbs and whatnot to be sewed back on?" In a situation like that you'd think you'd have to call, like, your closest friend to go looking for it. Like that one person you might count on to bail you out of jail in the middle of the night. "Yeah, your best man," one guy said. But size does become paramount because you want to just be able to say, "You can't miss it." I mean, when they walk in the room you want it to be the first thing they see. And, God forbid, you lose it outside. I mean, it's really got to stand out. "You know with me I'm just an average Joe," one guy confessed, "And if you're talkin' two-thirds, and they have to go by my description, people are gonna be out there picking up cigarette butts."

Dear Gangster: *What do you think about people you meet for the first time who have to tell you what type they are or aren't? I met this guy and was just talking about the lake I grew up near and he has to interrupt to tell me, "I'm not really the lake type." I said, "What are you, the water cooler type?" He says, "I like other types of water." I* said, "Well, why don't you type like a river and keep moving, baby child." The nerve of some people. Not the "lake type."

—Typesetter

Dear Typecasted: Yeah, what is it with the types lately. I think three people this week had to tell me they're "not really the Jay Leno type." What are they trying or not trying to tell us by typing themselves with bodies of water and late night talk show hosts. Are we trying to narrow ourselves down the only way we know how? Are we gonna keep it up until we all fit into one of three neat categories?

A.   *The I like freckles on breasts, malted milk balls, tuna without mayo just light seasonings type.*

B.   *The I only like* Godfather I *and* II *but not* III *because of Sophia, "1000 yd." mint floss, I hate phone mail type.*

C.   *The yeah,* The X-Files *is pretty good, what's wrong with ordering a tropical drink at my age, I couldn't live without my phone mail type.*

Dear Gangster: *What am I to her? Sometimes I believe I'm dependable and earnest and funny and trustworthy. But those are all in my head. What does she see? I can't stop thinking about this.*

—In My Head

Dear Donkey Boy: You are right not to listen to yourself. Because even in the most mundane situations it doesn't matter how we think of ourselves, does it? We can stop at a street corner and ask someone for directions and you can see in the way they approach that you're being sized up very quickly. It doesn't matter that in your head you're this person who doesn't want to be late for an appointment because it will inconvenience everyone else or that you love animals and small children and on this very day you worried about a plant. He may not see the man that worries about a plant. He may step off the curb, get a whiff of your Carefree sugarless bubble gum, note your pointy side-burns and send you down that road which dead ends at a recycling plant which happens to be closed and the only way out is in reverse up a one way road for 2.4 miles. That's a lot of neck craning. Anyway, I think it's safe to say that no one ever knows who they are until someone else decides at any given moment. Which may be the only reason life is interesting. In your case, I think your woman (like all women) fluctuates between two images of her man. The one being this charming fella who even seems to have sort of a Tom Jonesish Welsh accent when he first wakes you in the morning and the other being of donkey boy in *Pinocchio*.

Dear Gangster: *I've done a couple of things in the past that I'm certainly not proud of but my partner uses them on me every chance he gets. I tell him the past is the past and those things don't matter anymore but I guess if they matter to him then they matter, right?*
  —Past Lives

Dear Past Lives: You can tell yourself the problem is the past and agonize over it and think about what you could have done differently or what you could have denied or kept secret or pinned on someone else. Or you can tell yourself the problem is the present and get rid of the guy.

Dear Gangster: *My wife keeps telling me that because I'm a man and act like a man and behave like a man that she'll outlive me by a decade. "Men don't know how to live properly," she says. "They've yet to learn that from women." Is this true?* **—Manlike**

Dear Manlike: She's so full of it. The only reason women live longer than men is because they always sit down when going to the bathroom. You compare how many times they get off their feet for a break during a typical day to how you stand on your aching soles over a urinal and it's pretty obvious. Over a lifetime those mini-vacations easily add up to the six or seven years they've got on us now.

Dear Gangster: *Big Problem! I've been going out with my boyfriend for five years and recently I've developed a crush on another guy. Well, some friends thought it would be fun to let the other guy know and let's just say his reaction was very favorable. Now I'm going out of my mind. I think of him at work, with friends, when I sleep, eat, walk, talk, and worst of all, when I'm with my boyfriend. What should I do? I hope to someday marry my boyfriend when we're financially set but in the meantime should I have a fling or should I break up with my boyfriend and risk losing everything?*

—My Crush is Driving Me Crazy

Dear My Crush: The fact that you even use the word crush shows you're naive but the fact that you're ready to marry this guy when you're financially set even though you work, eat, and sleep another guy makes you a very up-to-date, mature, '90s woman. So how do we minimize your risk? There's no sense in leaving your boyfriend because you'd just end up doing the same thing to the new guy a few years from now, it's an endless cycle. That's why people get married, so they can stop. I got it. A win-win situation. You stop thinking about yourself. Stop being so selfish. Let's think about the new guy for a change. We both know he'd love to get his hands all over you. The thought's been planted and this poor guy has to eat and sleep, too, you know. Just let him have his way with you. Once, maybe twice, depending on how unselfish you're feeling. Tell him right up front that there can never be any more than this, just unbridled sex in brightly lit places. Your heart is taken and waiting to be financially set, but your body is his. Once, maybe twice. I'm betting you both can live with that. Oh, and you don't have to thank me for this advice . . . but he does.

Dear Gangster: *I got a problem . . . I'm thirty-one years old and attracted to a twenty-five-year-old man. We have both admitted that we like each other. (So you're saying, "So what's the problem?") Well, I really want this to blossom into a relationship and possibly marriage. You know what I mean. I can't screw this one up. I don't want to rush anything, but I don't want to lose anything either. I know you're saying, how can you lose what you never had? I've prayed to God that He send me a husband and if He's answering my prayers I really don't want to blow it.* **—My Mom Is Praying Too**

Dear Praying Too: This is huge. You're saying that God might have actually sent this guy and plopped him on your doorstep or the bar stool next to you or whatever for the sole purpose of becoming your husband. I gotta be careful here too 'cause you're, like, saying God already did His work and now I'm coming in like a consultant of the highest order. Do you think He knows you've come to me with this? Let's just say He does. So now you're problem isn't this guy anymore. Do whatever you want with him, you have my blessing, especially if he's financially set. But your real problem is the wrath of God for going over His head on this one. My advice: Run. And keep running. He's everywhere but He's really slow, man. He could be like in the kitchen and it might take Him a week to ten days to catch up to you in the master bedroom. Just keep on the move. Eat light, when sleeping wake yourself up every two hours and move to a different room, keep the movies you rent at about eighty-eight minutes.

SAY YES TO THE BIG BREAKFAST

Dear Gangster: *My boyfriend's never taken drugs or even touched alcohol and now all of a sudden he's a pothead. He works on the fringe of showbiz. Actually, he makes custom eyeglasses and some of his clients are celebrities. What happened is this one person (a defunct talk show host) gave him some pot as sort of a tip and he was thrilled. When I told him he was behaving ridiculously he only scoffed. "You don't understand," he said. "This is 'star pot.'" How do I bring him back down to earth?* **—Star Tripper**

Dear Tripper: It's funny that you would ask me this particular question because I know absolutely nothing about drugs EXCEPT that it's true what they say about celebrity pot. It's the best.

Dear Gangster: *This isn't the biggest deal but I'm sick and tired of my husband bragging about his chili. It's always, "You have to try my chili. It's the best. There's nothing like my chili." And even though his chili is only "O.K." the word starts to spread and when we go to a party it's always, "Oh Shelly, did your husband bring his chili? I've been telling everybody how great it is. Everybody! Shelly's husband makes the greatest chili." I'm sick of it. Should I just continue to go along with this charade?*   **—Chillied Out**

Dear Chillied: There's an important lesson there. It depends on the man. If this is a guy who's really makin' it in life, I mean, if he's the type who manufactures fancy bifocals and sells them for $4,500 a pop and people like Wil Shriner are always throwing him joints then, NO, you tell him his chili sucks and bring him down a notch. But, if he's the type who drives a Ford Escort, always comes home to his family at a decent hour, occasionally brings you flowers from the grocery store, and gives the dog a bath while he waits for his Weed Wacker to recharge, the answer is YES, you give him what you can. If it's the world's greatest chili trophy so be it. It's one of the few honors we decent guys have to reach for.

Dear Gangster: *I've already told my guy that I'm not free falling with him but he insists on doing it. "It's not dangerous," he says, "we'll be piggy-backing." I don't even know what he's talking about but I'm not doing it. When I tell him it's too dangerous he says, "Come on, when your time is up your time is up." Do you believe that?*

                    —I Don't Want to See the Treetops

Dear Treetops: A guy can't even brag about his chili, drop out of the sky, or smoke some famous dope anymore without causing a stir. Anyway, as far as time being up, again, I think it depends on the person. If he's only going to do it once and then go back to his job as a strip-mall manager, that's fine. But take that bungee cord instructor who plunged to his death recently after jumping out of a hot air balloon. Do you think his time would have been up if he hadn't decided at some point to make a career out of being a human yo-yo? In the words of the great Mcaulay Culkin, "I don't think so."

Dear Gangster: *I've always had these real high requirements for the guys I dated but the relationships never seem to last. Now I've reached the point where I'm ready to settle for a regular guy. Is that so bad?* **—Ready for a Joe**

Dear Joe Ready: What do you mean a regular guy? Somebody who brushes his teeth and actually stands around in the shower waiting for the conditioner to work? Someone who pats the heads of small children as he walks through a crowd? Just what do you mean? Someone who's had a "Humor in Uniform" tidbit almost published in *Reader's Digest*? Someone who plans his vacation to Dollywood two years in advance? Someone who doesn't bother to cut his sandwich in half? No, I don't know what you mean by a regular guy. Do you mean someone who's a civil service worker? Are you looking for a freakin' postman to ring once? Someone who doesn't like to drink but drinks two beers a day to raise his life expectancy? Someone who will make love to you for seven minutes right after Full House every other Friday night? Someone who's not good enough for you but you'll settle for in 1991? Someone you can use for forty years, buy plots with and rest in peace, shoulder to shoulder, for all eternity? What do you mean by a regular guy?

Someone you'll never love?

Dear Gangster: *I've got a problem with our best friends, Jan and Steven. We've been getting together with this couple in our building almost every weekend. Sometimes we go out but most of the time we just sit around, drink champagne as usual, and watch old movies. The other night though, things got out of hand. Somehow my boyfriend got the idea that Steven was making a pass at me and there was a bit of a fight. Now everyone is fighting. Even Jan won't look at me 'cause she says, "What's wrong with me that he wants to screw you?"*

—What Is Wrong?

Dear Tiny Bubbles: Champagne as usual? What kind of people drink champagne like it's a normal beverage? Champagne is something that you clean up half full glasses of after a wedding reception. You take a sip and run from champagne. Why do you think they smash boats with it and let it spill into canals? Why do you think they put it in those tiny glasses? Because no one drinks it. You'd have to be crazy to sit around guzzling champagne. What are you drinking it out of, old peanut butter jars? I think everyone needs to be forgiven. Steven sounds to me like he's just a "regular guy." You can't hold the average Steven responsible for who he wants to screw when he's got a brain full of bubbles. You're lucky he didn't go after the dog or the parakeet for God's sake. I'd be nuts on champagne. I'd be masturbating into the early chapters of romance novels, before I even really got to know the characters. I'd be fondling the people on crosswalk signs. Jesus.

Was it cheap champagne?

Dear Gangster: *I was with this girl for the first time the other night and she tells me that she could really get passionate with someone like me. But then she just stops and says it would be too risky. I'm harmless, I said. Then she called me a dangerous man. What's going on? One second there's passion, then I'm a risk, then I'm admittedly harmless, then I'm a dangerous man.*

—Lacking Identity

Dear Identity: I don't want to make matters worse or twist your guts into a poodle balloon but I've got a sneaky suspicion that you're just a "regular guy."

Dear Gangster: *Lately there's been a change in the way my boyfriend acts towards me. We'll be sitting on a couch right next to each other and it feels like he's clear across the room. Or we'll be driving down the highway and it feels like he's in the car in the next lane or the one behind me or in front of me or the one going the opposite direction or . . . oh, he's just got me so mixed up. I'm trying to figure out what I've done or haven't done. This is the third time this has happened to me in as many relationships, I might add. Seems to kick in around month number four. What's this all about?* **—Driving Alone**

Dear Driving: Sex. I don't know why I'm always the last one to figure things out but that's what it's all about—sex.

Dear Gangster: *We work late in my office and there's this one woman who always wants someone to walk her out to her car when she's ready to go. Now, I've sat here and watched her get walked out by several different men but she never picks me. I'll even volunteer when I see her start to get ready and she always says, "Oh, no, I've got a few more things to do here, thanks." And then she starts shuffling pa-*

pers until some other Tom, Dick, or Harry comes by and she shoots out the door. Why would she treat me this way?

—I'm an Ordinary Harmless Fellow

Dear Fellow Loser: It's about sex. Everything is. You wouldn't want to walk her out if you didn't want to have sex with her and she wouldn't refuse if she weren't so turned off by you sexually. That's it in a nutshell and I hate to even use that expression. Sex is the answer. Somebody asks, what time is it? The answer is sex. Somebody asks, why do circus acts bow after every little move they make even if it's as minor as handing somebody a stick to spin a plate on? The answer is sex. If somebody sincerely wants to know why there are 3,412 different kinds of breakfast cereal on the market, I don't know. But if they ask how come no matter how many cereals they add each year they still all fit in the same aisle at the grocery store the answer is sex.

Dear Gangster: *Why must I always be involved with big women who have small voices?* **—I Can't Hear Her**

Dear Hear This: SEX.

Dear Gangster: *I have a job most guys dream about. All day long I am surrounded by beautiful and exotic women. So why is it I'm so uncomfortable around them and have even come to find them despicable?* **—I Take That back about Despicable**

Dear I Take That back about Despicable: Smart move. And I don't have to tell a smart guy like you what the problem is. Sex. In your specific case it probably begins with your uneasiness with your own sexuality and how you sometimes feel sexless in a world that's based on sex. I know this fact has been around for centuries so I don't know why it's suddenly news to me, but it is. If it's news to you then it's sex to me, isn't that what they say? Or, if it's sex to you it's news to me. Anyway, that's it in a nutshell and all of a sudden I can't use that expression enough. It's like I've been saving it till the day I realized everything is about sex. Are any of them Tahitian?

Dear Gangster: *If deep down in my soul I'm . . .*

Dear You: Don't give me this soul crap. If you want to be right up front, if you want to be honest, just tell me it's about sex because that's what I'm gonna tell you. It's about sex.

Dear Gangster: *Of all the people I've dated in the last year . . .*

Dear You II: Sex. The answer is sex. It always has been. And the funny thing is nobody even has sex anymore and still that's what it's all about.

   Why is that?

Dear Gangster: *I've been going to the same therapist for the past three years. I started going because all of my relationships had gone from lasting about three days to about forty-five minutes each. I sought professional help after they started to dip below the ten minute mark. That's less than it takes cheese to melt in my old microwave. Anyway, after three years and about $9,500 (the company paid about fifty-three percent) the guy sits up in his chair. I swear to God this is the only time he ever sat up straight, not even during the*

highly detailed descriptions of my sexual escapades did he once get on the edge of his seat. Anyway, he's sitting there like he's just been hit with a lightning bolt or he's just found out about ATM cards or something. His expression is one of revelation. And then he says it, "I have your answer. It just hit me. A big breakfast. Every day. A big breakfast every single day of your life. Yes." That was it. $9,500 later.

—What Ever Happened to
"You Hated Your Mother Didn't You?"

Dear What Ever Happened?: I'm going with it. People have been telling me that my whole life. I'm telling you, he's right. It's time to say YES to the big breakfast. All my life I thought I was Mister Smartass Know-It-All and all the people pushing the big breakfast were fools. But yes, I'm saying YES to the big breakfast.

Dear Gangster: *I'm never gonna change. I'm always gonna leap into love and then inch my way out little by little. My last lady told me I started to smell like axle grease the week after we moved together. I was already preparing to shimmy out of another relationship like a creepy little worm-man. She's right. I'm never gonna change.*

—Greased Up and Ready to Go, Again

Dear Greased up and Ready: Hold the (cellular) phone and put some of that grease in the big ol' cast-iron frying pan. It's time for a big breakfast, my man. And I'm not just talking Sunday. A lot of you fools think Sunday is the day for the big breakfast. But no, I mean every day for the rest of your life. You're never gonna change. Pass me the blueberry syrup, you joker.

Dear Gangster: *I think I wrote you before about giving up. I was almost gonna kill myself when you told me to and then I didn't* *want to because you told me to. Do you mind changing your mind so I can go back to my original plan?*

—**Please, Please, Mr. Gangster Man**

Dear Please Pass the Silver-Dollar Pancakes: The plan is changed again, my friend. Two words: big breakfast. And in a case like yours I'm not talkin' toast and two over easy. I'm talkin' Belgium waffles, Denver omelettes, two hundred Jimmy Deans in the shape of a log cabin, hash browns, but not just hash browns as you know them but the eighteen different kinds of hash browns you get every time you try to order the hash browns that you like, and juice is the key—in one of those big glass pitchers like you only see on TV. Every morning you're a J.V. football team on game day, you're alive and hungry and ready to conquer the world right after the cheerleaders feed you a big breakfast. A big breakfast—tell me it's not infectious. Tell me right now, right this second, you don't want to live forever.

Dear Gangster: *It seems like "I love you" isn't enough anymore. I'm looking for something else to say but I can't find the words. Is there anything that means more?* —**Anything?**

Dear Anything: Is this a setup? Big breakfast. Big breakfast. Big breakfast. You want to love. You want to thrive. You want to make magazine models pop off the page and into your bed and make you a big breakfast afterwards. Have a big breakfast first. And wash the pans so the models don't know you've already eaten.

Dear Gangster: *My boyfriend and I had been to-gether for six months and everything was grand until one night in the kitchen we were arguing and I said something I shouldn't have. He freaked, threw his hands in the air and took off screaming. "That's it, you can't take that back, that's it!" I thought he'd be back for sure, but it's been two weeks now. What is this, one little slip, and the love of my life flees my kitchen forever?*

—Slipped in the Kitchen

Dear Slipped: My God, what did you say? This is bad. You know what this is, don't you? It's the SOME THINGS WERE SAID scenario. Sometimes this happens and there's absolutely nothing you can do. I had a friend who slipped in the bedroom. She had the perfect relationship with this guy for almost a year and one morning, innocently, while he was shaving in the bath-room, she mentioned how the dent he left in the mattress was ex-actly like Brian's. You don't need to know who Brian is but, believe me, she shouldn't even have been mentioning his name, let alone the cavern he had left in her mattress. Anyway, he looks in the mirror and she's patting the sheets, his nest for the past year, and he just blew. Out the door he went, half his face cov-ered with shaving cream. All she was left with was half of a man's morning whiskers floating in her sink. Pitiful. She tried to call, but you know what he said, "SOME THINGS WERE SAID." And you can't blame him. You can't just change the sheets after something like that. You can't expect a man to wake up every morning of his life wondering how many other men could match his dent. Wondering if his dent is no more remarkable than that of a hundred Brians, or a thousand Andrews, or a million Nor-mans. Having to open his eyes and face the fact that he is not ca-pable of leaving a mark of his own. My God, what did she expect?

Dear Gangster: *While my wife was away on business I decided, without telling her, to take a little trip of my own to visit some friends I hadn't seen since we went on a mountain retreat with the company I used to work with. We had scaled walls together, climbed out to the edge of the cliffs, jumped off telephone poles. You wouldn't believe what it did for our company spirit. I quit a couple of weeks after we got back though so I thought this would be a good chance for a reunion and just drink beer. To make a long story short, my wife beat me home and didn't understand how I could do that. She doesn't trust me now because . . . why?* **—A Free (Company) Spirit**

Dear Spirit: Because SOME THINGS WERE DONE. All you have to do is show your true colors once and you're always capable of being a sneaky conniving untrustworthy spouse. I had a roommate once who, during courtship and a fit of catastrophic proportions, raised a knife to his fiancé. It was a butter knife and had orange marmalade on it at the time, but it was a knife nonetheless. His little lady ran home screaming, "Daddy, Daddy, he pulled a knife on me." Well, of course, they kissed and made up two days later but the incident haunted him for years.

"How could you marry that son of a bitch, after he pulled a knife on you?" You can just imagine. They had plastic cutlery at the wedding. And for the first few years they were married he wasn't allowed near any of the children at family gatherings. It's only been recently that he sees the positive side to all this. He said, "After you're married for a while and feel like your life is over it's nice to have something like a switchblade story in your past." He figures he's gonna have his grandkids mesmerized: "Yeah, I remember the morning I pulled a knife on your Grandma." A few generations and he'll be a legend. So what'd you do, forget to tell the missus you were going somewhere? That's not much to work with but time has a way of exaggerating things. Maybe some of that telephone pole jumping stuff will get mixed in over the years and who knows? Relax and let it roll for a few generations. You could come out as a hero in all of this.

Dear Gangster: *In the end, do you think we all fall in love with the wrong person for the right reasons?*

—**Almost Sure**

Dear Almost: When all is not said and done, yes.

LOVE IN AN OFFICE BUILDING

Dear Gangster: *I'm so mixed up about this sexual harassment thing at work. I walk around speaking in half sentences now because I think something is going to slip out. I feel my outgoing personality will eventually be misunderstood. Whose rules are we playing by now anyway?*

—So, What Are You Doing after Work?

Dear What Are You Doing: I can't really address your situation in particular because for all I know you may be a real scumbag. But I was a bit shocked when we had a seminar on sexual harassment at work a few weeks ago and there at the top of the "Don't Rules" was staring, followed by following, leading up to brushing against. I'm always staring at people, regardless of sex. I have this nightmare of getting called into my supervisor's office and he lays out all these signed affidavits from all the people I've stared at in the last year and a half. And, as far as the following goes, there was that one incident with the temp I followed out to her car. I was sort of going that way anyway when I decided to follow her because she looked like she might have a big car. Most of the women I know have little cars and I was curious if she just might be a different kind of woman. A woman who drives a big car. I've followed people for things like this before but this was the first time any of them ever turned around abruptly and said, "Are you following me?"

I immediately said, "No," but had kind of a goofy smile on my face at the same time because she had just stopped in front of a big Chrysler. "Nice car," I said.

"I saw you staring at me earlier," she said.

"Oh, no," I said, squeezing past her, "that's my car right over there." As I pointed, I think my arm brushed against her hair.

Dear Gangster: *There is this guy at work who always gets so close to me when he has something to say that he, like, violates my air space. What's with him?*   **—Too Close to Call**

Dear Too Close: Men have this thing about a woman's breath. It boils down to the fact that it's the most personal thing they can violate without getting arrested. This one guy I knew constantly got off on women's exhalings. It was like a fetish the way he'd corner a girl, ask her a million questions, inhale every word she'd say, and then come around and brag about it. "You see that girl over there," he's gasp. "I got so much of her inside of me I'm gonna bust." I'll never forget the time we were carpooling into the city and there was this girl we saw jogging every day. We always called her "the most beautiful jogger in the city." Anyway, it was cold so she had white breath pouring out of her and this guy couldn't help himself. He jumped out of the car and just started swimming in it. He stopped her and she was huffing and puffing on him and he was just in a cloud of ecstasy. The next day he does the same thing, only this time he takes a handful of balloons out of his pockets and she starts blowing them up for him right there on the street. He hands her some money and jumps back in the car. We said, "What the hell?" He said, "I'm gonna sell balloons filled with 'the breath of the most beautiful jogger in the city' to guys at the office." We said how much? He said, five bucks. Anyway, you wouldn't believe what a hit they were. Bigger than rock gardens. Everybody had one, and the air in them was considered sacred, not to be released unless something really bad happened, like getting fired. That's when you'd need the sweet breath of a woman to revive your spirits. It got so we didn't even have to use the word fired anymore. It would be like, "Is Marty O.K.? I hear they're reworking his whole department," and all we'd have to do is shake our heads and say, "He's in there right now sucking down the breath of the most beautiful jogger in the city."

Dear Gangster: *Looking for a holiday gift for a fella that works in my office. I don't want him to think I'm swooning but I'd like to send the subtle message that I'm interested.*

—**One Lusty Elf**

Dear Lusty: How 'bout the ordinary balloon with a simple card that says, "Don't suck on this until you get fired."

Dear Gangster: *People are starting to act like I want something from them. The other day this hunky guy in the office dropped a bunch of stuff and I helped him pick it all up and then he looked at me* like, "Oh, now she thinks I should find her attractive and ask her out to dinner. Well, not in her dreams." He can go to hell. God knows I want something from somebody but not him. **—How about You?**

Dear How about Me: I had something completely un-like what you're talking about happen to me the other day. I'm driving out of the parking lot and this attractive woman, whom I've never seen before, has her car window down (I don't know what the hell she was doing with her window down) and smiles and waves as my car approaches hers. I wave back. I go home. I sleep well. The next day I'm sitting at my desk going over some figures (making up odometer readings for my expense report) and there she is standing over me. "Excuse me," she says (a lot less attractive out of her car by the way). "But I just wanted you to know I wasn't waving at you yesterday. You have the same car as a friend of mine. I just wanted you to know that."

"Why?" I said.

"Just so you know is all," she said.

"What are you saying?" I said. "You came over here to take back a wave?"

"I don't know you," she said.

"No, you don't," I said. "And I'm not the kind of person who tolerates someone who goes around taking back waves. Did I tell you I slept well last night?"

"Well, I hope it wasn't on account of my wave," she said.

"What about the smile, do you want that back too? Huh?"

"Did I smile? I didn't even kn . . ."

"Let me tell you exactly what you did," I said. "You saw a car approaching you that you thought was one of your close acquain-tances who deserved one of your waves and then you rolled your window down—God knows why. I can't remember the last time I saw someone roll a window down in this town. And then you waved and smiled and evidently wrote down my description in order to track me down today while I'm concentrating on falsifying my expense report and all of this just so you can take back the wave . . . and the smile at this point, I presume. That's it. From what I can tell that's all of it. Now, do you want it all back? You can have it all back. How's that? None of this happened. I didn't even sleep well last night as far as you're concerned. Okay, it's all yours. You can take it all back and walk away right now."

She walked away.

Later I saw her in the parking lot. I waved and she gave me the finger.

I slept well.

Dear Gangster: *No one is paying any attention to me anymore. When I first started working at this place guys were always asking me to go to lunch or, at the very least, take a fifteen minute break to talk over a problem or something. Now, nothing. I eat alone. I break alone.* **—I Am the Alone One**

Dear Alone One: No one's been talking to me lately either but I've been playing this new game at work called "Everyone Is Trying to Impress Me." If someone stops by a desk near mine to talk to someone else it is only in the hopes that I will overhear and find them interesting. If someone mentions they bought a new dress I immediately picture them pushing hangers through the racks to find that one particular dress they believe will please me. I can hear them snapping at the sales clerk, "No, no, no. I'll know it when I see it." Someone could walk in this office right this second and hold up the keys to a brand new car and I would naturally assume that they spent the $15,678 in hopes the sporty little number might catch my eye. I like getting in this mind set. It's a real booster. Oh, look at her making extra copies at the Xerox machine. Everyone knows she only needs two copies of that report but she's making ten because the machine is in my line of view and she thinks sooner or later I have to look up and notice that provocative stance she's been trying to sustain for the last eight minutes. It's sad.

Dear Gangster: *Got one for ya. My buddy and I were discussing how long we can keep a woman's attention. Sometimes we time each other to see who can talk to a woman longer. Sometimes it's even a contest. In this one particular case, right after he had talked to a woman for seven minutes, I walked a woman out to the parking lot. The lot is two blocks away from the office and an eleven-minute stroll counting elevator time and all. He says that doesn't count. If anything it should count half. Whaddaya say, my man?*   **—Tick Tock**

Dear Tick: I guess what he's saying is, holding a woman rapt within arm's length for seven minutes is a lot tougher than moving at a pedestrian pace with a particular destination, such as a parking lot, in mind. But, we have to know some things. Were you just tagging (schlepping) along out to her car or were you going to your car at the same time? Now, if she was walking you to your car and then had to turn around and walk four blocks in the other direction to get to her wheels then I'd say we double *your* time. You see I need to know the whole story. And what about the pace? Was it a "let's get the hell out of this office" kind of pace or was it like I'll watch your legs and you watch my legs and we'll match each other stride for stride? 'Cause if you had to work at it, I mean, glance at those calves balancing on those black spikes and then look up quick to make the obligatory eye contact and then make conversation at the same time, well . . . Were there any stops? Did you have to hold the elevator doors open or press anyone else's number? You didn't go stupid on her and try to fill the holes in the conversation by announcing things like a little kid as you passed by them? You didn't go like "Aaaaaa, hot dog cart. I like hot dogs. Yeah I was thinking . . . Aaaaaaaa, fire hydrant. Used to like to jump them. Hey, penny flattening machine. When I was a kid I used to put pennies on the railroad tra . . ." If you did, deduct ten minutes. Was there any waving? That could go both ways. I mean, it would be nice if other people saw you as a couple leaving the building. But then if they waved to you guys, called you by your nicknames, and only she waved, and it was almost like waving them over, like a splashing around in open sea save-me-from-this-creep-type of wave that's one thing. Or if they only waved to you and called you Mr. So and So, and you gave a slight professional nod without averting your eyes from the calves and gave out a signal that said, "Yes, I see you, but please, I'm with this attractive woman now. I'll certainly see you tomorrow and give you all the details," that's another. And if, and this is a big glorious if, if neither of you responded to numerous waves, if in fact you were both oblivious to all waving, if you were moving along in your own private cloud immersed in each other's lives and it wasn't until you were halfway home that you remembered you had a bet going and had to retrace your steps and struggle to recollect exactly how many minutes you spent with this woman, then, my friend, that is something very special indeed.

Dear Gangster: *I was going to surprise my girlfriend with a trip to Hawaii but some of her friends told me you can't just spring something like that on someone. I'm afraid I'm going to plan this great trip and she may only get upset with me. Should I change my strategy?*
—**Packed Bags**

Dear Packed: Do it. She'll be in shock but it'll be worth it. A co-worker of mine's husband recently planned a surprise trip to Memphis for their anniversary. He didn't tell her a thing. He just came into work one morning and said, "Follow me darlin', we're going to the airport." You should have seen her face. And every one at the job knew what was going on and we all got up and started cheering as he carried her out the door. It was just like the end of *An Officer and a Gentleman*. And after they were gone we all went back to sewing.

Dear Gangster: *Is there a new thing going on out there called "building?" Like you build me up and I'll build you up and we'll both have enough confidence to maybe poke our heads out into the real world. I work with these two girls at work who are constantly stroking each other's egos. You think this is good? Should I get in on this? Can I? I'm sure they'd have some nice things to say about me if I threw a few compliments their way.*
—Please

Dear Please: I insist. This "building" as you have so aptly named it is just what we need to get us through the '90s. I watched a case of it the other day that was totally mesmerizing. I was having a couch delivered and the two guys moving it in had "building" down. They were like the original building blocks. The conversation went something like this as they carried the couch past a mirror in the living room.

Steve: Stop! Look at you, Larry. Just take a good hard look. I mean, seeing you at the other end of a couch is one thing but see-ing your reflection. I could just . . .

Larry: You're looking very upright yourself there, my man. You look like something God . . . No, forget God. You look like something a woman would create. I mean what did God know about what women wanted, right? But if a woman had created exactly what she wanted in a man to fill all her desires I believe it would be an exact replica of what's standing at the other end of this couch.

Steve: I have to disagree with you, my friend. I believe God is a woman and you are her fantasy.

Larry: I'm God's fantasy.

Steve: How do you shave? How do you get up and look at that face without being distracted? I mean, I've just gotten used to you face to face, but your reflection . . . Move up a little, move up a little I want to be out of the picture. Make it so we can only see you in the mirror. There, there.

Larry: Please, you're gonna make me blush.

Steve: You mean you're not blushing already? That is your natural color?

Larry: That's enough. Back up, back up. If there should be two of anybody in this room it should be you. Look at that. What woman could resist that? Think of the most innocent and pure woman you've ever met, the most honest like . . . like who's the matriarch of the Osmond family? Who's the mama?

Steve: I can think of everybody's names but not the parents: Donny, Marie, Jimmy. Wasn't there even a Dale? Man, I can't think of the mother's name. You know, that's not right. They should have been thanking her on every talk show when they were big. It should be on the tip of all our tongues. 'We owe it all to our Mom, Golda. No, Let me think, 'We owe it all to our Mom, Helen,' No. 'We owe it all to . . .'

Steve: Mary. Let's call her Mary. That's a simple and pure name and let's say she'd been a faithful and loving wife for forty-seven years and she walked in this room right now. I am telling you, she could not resist the two of you. I'm not saying whether her eyes would go straight to the reflection first or right on your flesh. That's anybody's guess. But I'm saying she would belong to you.

Larry: Man, you were cookin' there and now you got me paired up with the Osmond's old lady. Man, wipe that out. Wipe that out.

Steve: You know what I'm saying. Hypothetically, right? The whole concept of . . .

Larry: Let's just get the couch down. We need a couple of seconds to forget that one. That was sloppy. There, he wants it over there. Just a little further. Wait! Did you see that? The way the light . . . Of course you didn't see that. The way the light hit you I swear it was unearthly. My heart was racing. You were like a vision, man. I can't even hang around you anymore. What's the sense? How can I compete with you? Like an angel you look, like some kind of a Zen warrior, a vision. You are a vision. Put the two of us in a room and what are the ladies gonna go for, huh? I may be the great reflection but when it comes right down to it what are they gonna go for, huh? The Reflection or The Vision?

Dear Gangster: *I think this girl has had enough of me simply because I'm not able to take as leisurely a lunch as her. Sometimes I've stretched my break 'cause I'm crazy for her but I end up getting reprimanded by my boss. At her job she gets away with murder. I don't think they care if she ever comes back. But I've been warned too many times. I can't do it anymore. I told her so and she said, "Oooooo, I can't live like that." I don't want to lose but I have to be able to say*

—The Lunch Stops Here

Dear Lunch Stopper: I had this girlfriend, God bless her, who was the lunch scientist, the lunch expert. People actually called her "The Luncher." And not in a matter-of-fact way but like Harvey Keitel was "The Cleaner" in *Point of No Return,* that was the way she was considered "The Luncher." It was a term of total respect. I think the only reason she dug me was because I have very little responsibility in my life and could lunch with her endlessly. People used to laugh, saying we were the ideal match. "Look, The Gangster going out with The Luncher. That's perfect." Anyway, she was the master. The first thing she taught me was always leave fifteen minutes early for lunch. "No one looks to see if you're early going to lunch, only if you're late coming back." Also, she didn't think you should decide where to eat until you got in the car. But don't get her wrong. She did believe in spending the whole morning discussing where lunch would take place. That's O.K., just as long as you don't decide. "Because once people know where they're going to eat they start picturing the place and exactly where they're going to sit and what they're going to order, all those things that take up valuable time. So before you know it you're back in the car, lunch over." In her book there was nothing worse than setting yourself up for a short lunch. A couple of times she liked to break things down, like you get drinks at one place then a salad somewhere else then another for the main course and so on until you were sipping espresso looking over a glistening bay of water at your office building which was now about three desserts and 110 miles away. It was beautiful once in a while but she would go crazy with this stuff. We once got drinks at one place and straws at another. The best, the absolute best, was when we were in this Italian place and I ordered first and then when it was her turn she said, "Whoa, I'm not eating here." What? But I just . . . "Yes, you're eating here but I'm not." This was genius at work. She was experimenting. She would watch me eat lunch and then we would go some place else and I'd watch her eat lunch. Two lunches for the price of one. Two lunches, twice the time. Sheer genius. I liked watching her eat and I told her so. She didn't like watching me eat and she told me so. Things fizzled out after that.

Dear Gangster: *Well, I've been reading your columns and I decided to tell you my problem. I've liked this guy for over three months and now I want to try to get his attention, but I don't know how. Could you please tell me some ideas to try.*   **—Curious Susan**

Dear Sue: Attention Getters. I don't know. I'm not sure I'm the one who should give you advice on that. I once walked over to a woman I admired at work and started to go through her pocketbook. She jumped up laughing and started pulling at it. We had a little tug-of-war going, very playful, and went on to have some good times and a semi-meaningless relationship. But I've tried that stunt seventy-seven times since and have yet to have another positive reaction. I just keep telling myself, "It worked once, maybe it will work again. Maybe someday I'll be able to have one more semi-meaningless relationship that I trigger by pawing through a woman's purse." The thing is, when it does work, it's great—the tug-of-war, the stuff spilling on the floor, the laughter, the picking it up, the sex on her father's boat, the sex at her aunt's villa, the sex at her brother's pet store. If it worked once why wouldn't it . . .

Dear Gangster: *My boyfriend is just out of college and has his first real job with an accounting firm. He's real smart and doesn't have any problems with the job but he can't get used to wearing a suit. He's played around with numbers all his life but not in a suit. He really hates it. I mean, really. He comes home cursing at his clothes. He's usually half undressed by the time he gets in the house and he won't even sleep in the same room as his suits. How can I help him?* **—Unsuited**

Dear Unsuited: All I can say is he's doing the right thing by keeping the suits out of the bedroom. I have a close friend who works in real estate and he always dressed kind of casually but recently his boss started insisting he attend these social gatherings with local businessmen and of course, wear a suit. "I tried to get out of it," he said, "but times are tough you know. I don't want to make any waves so I put the suit on but it's like wearing me. It's sending me in different directions. It's making me pose when I'm just trying to stand still. And it's awkward the way it hovers around me, never really touching my body. It won't settle down. It won't rest. When I squirm around and try to get comfortable in it I feel like my body is running real fast back and forth trying to get away from it, like I'm making a dozen trips to get a quart of milk but I never have any milk to show for it, you know. It's a nightmare."

The poor bastard. I thought it was just a phase but every time I saw him he'd just go on and on like that. I met his girlfriend recently at a wedding and she said he's begun to swear it's giving him commands from the closet at night. "Sometimes he gets up and yells at it like a deranged ventriloquist would talk to his dummy," she said. "But, I guess everybody has their own little eccentricities. So, anyway, how've you been, rummage through anybody's purse in the last hour?"

Dear Gangster: *My girlfriend smokes. I don't. We both work in the same huge office in a no smoking building. The thing is, all the smokers huddle outside in the parking lot during the day and it seems everyone has become friends with my Hannah. When we walk through the building or go down in the elevator together all these strange men say hello to her and just ignore my presence. They wave and smile and when I ask Hannah who they are, all she can say is, "They're my smoker friends."* **—Outside the Smoke Ring**

Dear Outside: They are a close knit society unto them-selves, smokers are. Someone once told me that a smoker will talk to anyone who also smokes. Oh, and I can just see it now, "Hannah, Hey Hannah, Hannah Baby," and those little salute waves, hands sticking up like mailbox flags, and then when you're not looking they're pointing to their watches like, "It's al-most time for a cigarette break, darling." Because they know the habits of Hannah and she will be in the parking lot soon and they will have her all to themselves for the length of an entire cigarette while you sit inside . . . working, working, working. And it's not that you're worried about your doll's lungs turning black and be-ing awakened thirty years from now only to see her coughing up charcoal briquettes into a bucket on the night stand. No, it's the waving that's killing you, isn't it? There is nothing worse than be-ing the odd man out at the wrong end of a wave aimed at your woman. Someone once told me smokers will wave to anyone who smokes. I'm the type of guy that puts good health before anything, anything but love.

Start smoking or you'll soon be taking one deep breath as you lose her forever, man.

Dear Gangster: *Can you believe how many beautiful people there are around now? Look around. I can't remember when there were so many beautiful people around.*

—And I'm Not One of Them

Dear Not One: You know I'm staring at one of those peo-ple right now. And I have this little test I do to see how beautiful *I* am by timing how long it takes for them to stare back, if ever. Well, let's do a little test now, I'll keep staring and then print the results below, that way we'll know exactly where I stand in the big picture.

Seventeen minutes: She looked up abruptly but it wasn't me. Someone directly behind me dropped a cellular phone that screamed when it hit the ground. It's been so many places it thinks it's alive.

Forty-four minutes: She's looking my way but I think it's just part of the new eye exercise program she does after every three hours at the terminal. Her face is all distorted, but don't get me wrong, she's still beautiful.

One hour, nine minutes: She is looking at me like . . . like you wouldn't believe. Like I'm her favorite maître d', that's the look. Wait, she's getting up, I'm getting up, I'm gonna have to show her to her table, she's coming over, right this way ma'am. We are beautiful people. She's getting very close, I can see her lips forming, trying to shape an "s," I believe. It's as if she's going to say, "Show me," like show me the way, or "special," she wants the special. Here it comes, here it comes . . . "STOP STARING AT ME!"

Dear Gangster: *What's the absolute best way to meet some-one in an office building?*
                                                    —No Water Cooler

Dear Coolerless: I thought I really nailed it a couple of weeks ago. It was going to be the ultimate act of pre-planned spontaneity. I'd seen this women in the break room a couple of times but I had no idea what floor she worked on or what depart-ment. All I knew about her was that we would be perfect to-gether. (How do we get these ideas in our heads?) That, and she was always in the break room at irregular times, like late morning when everyone else is busy planning to split for lunch, or late af-ternoon when everyone is putting their sneakers on to run to their cars. So it's about 4:20 when I catch her at the vending ma-chines. I'd been checking the break room at two minute intervals since 4:00; 4:14, 4:16, 4:18, 4:20, bingo. I get behind her real fast and wait for, guess what?

THE SOUND OF A VENDING MACHINE'S REFUSAL OF A ONE DOLLAR BILL.

Now, I know she's easygoing, not one to be in a big rush, would probably take the time to stop and pet an organ grinder's monkey on the way to the hospital to see a grandmother that only had four minutes to live. She's a lot like me. But this just drives her nuts, it's maddening. That little sound it makes—vittttt, vittttt. It's such a buzz-off type sound, isn't it? And whose dollars did they make these things for anyway, Tony Randall's? Who the hell irons their money?

So, I'm behind her and I have to figure out how many chances to take before I pull out the dollar that I ironed the night before. I mean, I know it's going to spit it out on the first try, that's a given. That must just be to see, like, if it's green. You can hear the machine saying, "O.K., it's green, let them stick it in again and we'll check for the number one in the top right hand corner. O.K., now three more times for the rest of the corners. All right, did you see the eye over the pyramid on that try? Let 'em stick it in one more time just for an eye check." Anyway, I figure she knows once is mandatory too so I let it go—vittt, vittt. She kind of changes her stance a little. (Did I tell you that she dresses real nice but always wears comfortable shoes? Very sexy but down to earth, you know.)

"Are you sure your dollar has the eye over the pyramid?" I said. I think she giggled. Her shoulders wavered a little. (I always thought she was the type I'd probably be able to get a lot of giggles out of, but tough for a real hard laugh.) Then she took it and kind of rubbed it on her thigh to flatten it out. I wanted to see that again but I couldn't take any chances. There it goes, there it goes, slip it in, slip it in,—vittt, vi . . .

"Wanna trade?" I stepped up.

"Ooo, is that new?" she said, admiring my one dollar bill. "It's so smooth and . . ."

"No, no, I just slept on it," I said.

"Well, thanks," she said.

Vittt-ca-chung, and there was her York Peppermint Pattie. I had to move fast now. Step right up to bat. Vittt, vittt, vittt, vitttt, vitttt, vitttt, vitttt, vittt . . .

At the doorway she turns, "Geeez, don't you have a good dollar for yourself now?"

"Just slept on the one, but that's O.K., I . . ."

"No, here, take my change . . ."

She was already eating the mint, very nonchalant like. I immediately started saying, "No, no, no, I couldn't," but all I could think about was that Peppermint Pattie breaking open on her teeth and that mixture of deep dark chocolate and Crest Toothpaste flavor that's as refreshing as an alpine wind. I couldn't help but imagine how my tongue would feel like a skier in the Swiss Alps in her mouth, zig-zagging and free-styling and . . . God, I wanted to owe this woman money.

This was working out perfectly. It couldn't have worked any better had I planned it for six weeks instead of four. Of course I will take your money and then I will track you down some spring afternoon and we will make mad passionate love on top of the two quarters you thought you would never see again. And when we're through they'll be melted down like two coins left on the tracks while the midnight train passed through town.

"Helen!"

"Tyler, what are you doing here?"

Yeah, what the hell is he doing here? I've never seen this guy before. Suddenly I was the epitome of inconsequential.

"I was just gonna loan him some change to . . ."

"Oh you don't want a guy like this owing you money," he cracked. "How much you need there, bud?"

He didn't wait for an answer. He just crammed a pile of coins in my hands and took Helen by the arm. "So what is this, I hear you're a free agent now?"

As they headed out the doorway together the last thing I saw was her breaking off a piece of the pattie and sticking it in Tyler's mouth. He whispered something in her ear and she laughed.

Hard.

Dear Gangster: *I'm having a love affair with a woman at work. The strange thing is that we've never met. We write each other on e-mail or talk on the phone every day and we get along great. I'm seriously considering leaving California and moving to Ohio where she lives. I can't stop thinking about her! She's witty, intelligent, fun, and physically fit. Should I throw caution to the wind and make the big move?*

By the way, I'm unhappily married and have two kids.

—Columbus Bound

Dear Bound: I once mail-ordered a pair of x-ray glasses sight unseen. Very disappointed. But I'm hard to please. I think what you have to do is sit your family down in a small room and say very clearly, so even you can hear yourself, "I'm so unhappy I'm willing to leave all of you for someone I've never met."

By the way, how fit is she?

Dear Gangster: *I just go this new job, which is a pretty good job, but you have to wear a uniform. I get embarrassed when girls come around. I always feel like they must be thinking how goofy I look.*

—The Shoes Are Mine

Dear Shoes: Hey, the kid down the street from me works at McDonald's and when he comes by to invite me to these parties he has after his late shift he's always still in uniform—a couple of times he was even still wearing the drive-thru headset—and he's always got a nice young lady on his arm. Of course, his father owns a recording studio and the kid drives this car that looks like a rocket ship with dual testicles. In a more down-to-earth situation, a couple of women I work with are always fantasizing about men in uniform and I don't mean the armed forces type. They like to look across the office and pick out the perfect uniform for a guy. "He'd look good in UPS brown," one'll say. "No, he's too calm. I couldn't see him hustling that hard," the other says. "Maybe Federal Express, yeah, I could see him handling more envelopes than boxes. He's not a box man. He's more of an overnight envelope man. The 10:30 on the dot type." You see, the thing is, people put you into uniforms whether you like it or not. But lose the shoes, will ya? They don't match.

Dear Gangster: *There are so many people to know but if you take the time to know them you never get to know the people you don't have time left to know. I don't really believe in love at first sight. I have to get to know people and every day I feel like I might have let someone get by me when I should have stopped and gotten to know them because that's the only way you get to know people you otherwise wouldn't know, you know.*   **—Who Knows**

Dear Who Knows: I don't know but I think I know what you're talking about and time is a big part of it. We just don't have time. I once got a call in an office I used to work in and the person on the other line asked me if I knew one Kathleen Ritz. Now, I looked up and there was Kathleen about nine feet away at another desk. Here we were, working for the same company, sharing the same space five, sometimes six, times a week and I had to stop myself from simply laying down a cordial, "Yes," to the woman on the phone. It would have been a lie. Instead, I said, "Kathleen Ritz. Well, I can see her very clearly from where I'm sitting without my glasses and I could probably throw something at her and hit her square in the head but, 'Do I know her?' No, I don't know Kathleen Ritz." After I got off the phone I felt kind of strange about that, like it just wasn't right. Why hadn't Kathleen and I ever taken the time to get to know one another, even slightly? So I told Kathleen exactly what happened. (By computer message, of course.) And the reply I got back (by computer message, of course) said, "Do you want to know me? Do you want to know that I graduated from high school forty-seventh in my class? Do you want to know which one of my parents is still living? Do you want to know if I've ever had a new car? Do you want to know how many times I've been in love, *in the past year*? Do you want to know where I go to hide and every little thing in my life that makes me want to hide? Do you really want to know me?"

I said one more thing to her (by computer mess . . .) that was never even acknowledged but I think it was the most truthful answer I could have given her. I said, "Yeah, but could you make it quick?"

BEWARE OF REHAB LOVE

Dear Gangster: *My boyfriend, Ted, is about half-way through a drug rehabilitation program at a nearby hospital and he seems to be doing well but I wonder where I will fit in when this is all over. I never had a serious problem and I never knew him when he didn't.* **—Visiting Hours Are Almost Up**

Dear Almost: Beware of Rehab Love. If you had a problem too and you both went in together that would be a different story. Then the bond grows deeper. But if he goes in alone he'll find some fragile creature to mate with. And it doesn't matter in there—alcoholics hook up with bulimics, crack addicts fall in love with compulsive shoppers. Everyone latches on to someone they can call a robed "savior" in hospital issue and take home for the rest of their lives. That way they can both milk their rehabilitation and use it as an excuse for failing in every other aspect of life. "Honey, you're smacking the kids." "Yes but I haven't had a drink in four years." "Darling, this is the third job you've had in six months." "Sure, but it's also my fourth anniversary of not throwing up dinner." "I love you." "I love you too." "I'm so proud of you." "I'm so proud of you." "We're doing great, aren't we?"

Whether it's the Sober Ted or the Junky Ted you'll be forever on the outside. I can hear him telling his counselor about you now, "How can she ever identify with me, Doc?" And the counselor saying, "I'm not a real doctor but that's a good realization, Ted. I'm gonna give you a gold star for this session and put you down for an extra piece of cheesecake tonight. Your new girlfriend can't seem to keep hers down." As sorry as it sounds, by the end of six weeks in rehab, a previous romance is not just lost love but a mere hallucination. Start your own withdrawal now.

Dear Gangster: *My wife and I are pretty close with a couple a few houses down from us. Recently, the guy has really gone off the deep end with drugs and my wife thinks I should try to do something. I wouldn't even think of getting involved but it's starting to affect our relationship because my wife is always on the phone with his hysterical girlfriend. Plus, he's started to hit me up for money for you know what. My wife insists we have to do something to help. What do you think?*
—Don't Know My Place

Dear My Place: I'm gonna tell you right up front that you should definitely try to intervene with some professionals. But, what's the hurry? I got a cousin who worked his way through a similar situation with the finesse of a Weed Wacker. He had just moved into a house near a friend of his with a drug problem when he realized he had a problem too. He'd never had a lawn before and didn't realize everything a man needs to keep things tidy. His desperate junkie friend had it all—gas hedge trimmer, sit-down tractor, edger, blower, you name it. "Every time he'd run low on cash we'd walk over to his garage and I'd low-ball him on another essential," he said. "But the second his garage was empty I opened the phone book and dialed one of those 800 numbers to get him some serious help." Apparently everything went well after that and the guy got his drug problem under control with a little help from his good friend. I saw my cousin recently and he laughed, "I'm like the Black & Decker of rehabilitators. Yeah, the guy's all straightened out but his yard is a mess."

Dear Gangster: *I guess my new mother-in-law has been studying my habits. Last weekend she cornered me with the question: Do you have to drink to have a good time? I immediately, instinctively, honestly, answered, "YES." Is that a bad thing?* **—Cheers**

Dear Cheers: I opened this up to discussion among my colleagues by first asking, "Has anybody ever had a bad time while drinking?" We were all dumbfounded by immediately, instinctively, honestly, answering, "NO." Of course there are regrets and embarrassments on certain days after but when the actual drinking takes place good times seem to roll. I guess that's why drinking has been going on since the beginning of time and some of us try to make it a non-stop thing which brings us to the question is that a bad thing? Just to kind of test my own status I've made a vow in front of several people that I am not going to drink again until I have a good time not drinking. It's been about six days now and nothing so far, but I can wait. I have no problem waiting for a good time. I mean, it's just an off week, I'm sure on an on week I would have already had a good time and could get back to drinking so I don't have to leave it to stinkin' chance if you know what I mean.

Dear Gangster: *Hey, Gangster man. I got a beer problem. If I have beer in the house my boyfriend takes it for granted and never brings beer over. If I don't have beer in the house he buys some but then takes whatever's left home with him. If you don't have a solution it's O.K., he's not that important to me anyway.*

—Boyfriend or Beer, Boyfriend or Beer?

Dear B or B: I've got a solution that I think will give you just what you need. Smaller doses of your boyfriend and larger doses of beer. My Uncle Johnny always kept his beer beneath his bed under a wool blanket to keep it extra warm and would only put one at a time in the fridge as he drank them. That way, if someone stopped by he could say, "I'll get you a beer if you don't mind waiting around and talking to me for an hour while it chills." Of course no one would put themselves through an hour of Uncle Johnny for one stinkin' beer. Since you don't care that much about this guy anyway I suggest you tell him not to pick up any, you got it covered, and then one-at-a-time him to death. Pretty soon it'll just be you and your lager. Man, that sounds good.

Dear Gangster: *My girl is a dream except for the fact that she likes to steal. Or "swipe" as she puts it. Little things, like a toothpick holder off someone's coffee table, or like, well, the biggest thing she ever took was this lighter shaped like a Harley Davidson Sportster. It was kind of cool, pewter I think. Anyway, you think this is just a phase? I'm taking her to my parents' house this weekend.*

—Worrying about Mama's Knickknacks

Dear Hide That Emmet Kelly, Jr. from the Franklin Mint: Sounds like a phase you wanna phase out before you take her to meet the folks. I know a guy that got into a nasty situation at a restaurant a couple of months ago. He likes his beers to always be ice cold so he takes one of those can insulators everywhere he goes. Well, he gets up and goes to the bathroom and while he's gone they clear the table. The beer insulator is gone. So he goes up front and says, "Hey, where's my insulator?" and the guy goes, "Maybe it's the same place as the vase." So he says, "What the hell you talkin' about? If you think it's with the vase go get it." He tells me that the guy had a real attitude about it which got him kind of going and he started getting louder and louder: "I want my insulator!" The restaurant is in a hotel so finally this guy in a suit shows up, the house detective, and tells him there's the little matter of the vase. And he starts cracking up, "Vase? What is this, the Maltese Falcon? Who do I have to call, Barnaby Jones? I just want my beer insulator!" At that point the detective realized the guy really didn't know anything about the vase on the table that his girlfriend had stuck in her purse while he was in the bathroom. "And then when he told me, what could I say? I know Cindy. I mean, I don't just use her for sex. I know her as a person and I know her well enough to know she wouldn't think twice about stealing that vase. Anyway, I stuck up for her. I said, "Don't you ever accuse my Cindy of . . ."

You said, "My Cindy?" I said.

"Yeah, my Cindy, and I could see that they wanted a trade off but I wasn't going to have any part of it."

Dear Gangster: *I'm new in town and my social life was just picking up when I got arrested. It's just bad checks, no big deal, but they've put me under house arrest and I have to wear one of those*

*thingamajigs on my left ankle. How am I going to keep up with my
new friends?*
—**One Caged Woman**

Dear One Caged Woman: I love that by the way—
One Caged Woman. First thing I'd do if I were you is get a T-shirt
made. But listen, I had a friend, Cheryl, who had this problem
(just bad checks, no big deal) and it turned out to be a godsend.
She was a nobody until she got confined to her place. Right away
it was a curiosity thing. Everyone wanted to stop by and touch it.
"I call it Willard," she told everyone. "Because it rats on you if
you leave the yard." That always got a big laugh all around. She
must have said it when everyone was wasted. Anyway, she started
having parties at her house and pretty soon everyone was having
parties at her house. People would say, "I'm having a party. I'm
gonna have it at Cheryl's house. You know, so she can come." She
didn't seem to care and we had some great all-nighters. Usually
around midnight we'd pick her up like we were going to throw
her in a swimming pool but there was no pool. We'd carry
her kicking and screaming and toss her into the neighbor's yard
hoping to set off the rat. She would scramble back like an
Irish Setter wearing panty hose up to its collar. She looked beautiful. All the guys were crazy about her. I was in love. For
nine months she was the damsel trapped in the tower. The
Queen of the Convicts. But once her sentence was up and they
cut her loose the party was over. It was the end of an era for most
of us. I, for one, stopped returning her calls. An acquaintance
told me recently that she's a very desperate woman now. Writing
checks all over town. She just can't handle freedom after being at
the top for nine glorious months. The full name is Cheryl
Bergund for you shopkeepers out there. Beware. She's a desperate
woman.

Dear Gangster: *It just hit me that the guy I've been going out with has been stoned since the day I met him. Is that possible?*

—And He's So Much Fun

Dear So Much: There are some people, some good people, who only get high once but they keep it going for like . . . forever. Somebody has to love these people. Why not you? Let me know if the fun lasts forever too.

Dear Gangster: *My new boyfriend seems to get arrested for the silliest things (usually when he's drinking), like running over mail boxes on his bicycle or, get this one, causing a disturbance at a Laundromat. He only gets charged with something minor or has to pay for damages but these things keep happening. He's a really nice guy but is this going to escalate into more serious criminal activity?*

—Miss Demeanor

Dear Miss: I was constantly getting calls to bail out an ex-roommate of mine. Everybody used to call him "Gilligan." I don't want to try and top your Laundromat incident but let me list a few of the crimes he was actually taken in for. 1. "Overloading a pony." He had too much to drink at his nephew's birthday party and refused to get off the rented pony (maximum passenger weight 65 lbs.) until he could back it into one of the parking spaces in front of the town house. He failed to get the pony to go in reverse and the pony's manager had to call the cops. 2. "Mauling of a stuffed animal." He was going to an elevator when a guy, who only saw his son once a year, was coming out with one of those giant stuffed animals. "It looked like a cross between Yogi and Odd Job, scared the crap out of me," Gilligan said. Anyway, when it came at him he defended himself like any one would have and ripped it to shreds. Cost $275. 3. "Sleeping in a Mc-

Donald's cage" Had a few too many and sometime in the wee hours climbed into one of those McDonald's playgrounds with all the multicolored balls and fell asleep. "Like snoozing in a gumball machine," he said. Needless to say, when the morning shift came on they called the cops who were already outside waiting to get their Egg McMuffins. What I'm trying to get at is guys like this are a bit of a panic. They're sweet and bring a little excitement to your life. But then again, I'm not mating with one of these types. I mean, I wouldn't suggest having sex with someone like this even if he'd had three vasectomies and there was only one millionth of a chance he could reproduce. Even if he'd had his sex organ replaced with a small goose-neck lamp I wouldn't advise taking the chance. What I am saying is don't let a person like this touch you but he's good people to hang out with when you don't have time to get drunk yourself. In these hectic times we all need someone like that in our lives.

Dear Gangster: *My guy has a problem that may sound silly but has gotten quite serious. He was baby-sitting his neighbor's pets but they have so many he forgot about the itty-bitty finches. The neighbors came home to dead finches but they took it a lot better than my guy has. He's been dwelling on it ever since. It's affecting our relationship and friends say he's even falling behind at work because of this.*

—**Birdened**

Dear Birdened: He may recover but he can never have a relationship with you. He can't allow himself to care for anyone or anything ever again. You don't get a second chance in this little egg-shaped world of ours. Sorry. And please don't advise him to go to his boss and tell the truth of why his productivity is down. I had a partner who got a speeding ticket in a school zone and couldn't stop the pounding in his brain which constantly alerted him to the terrible, terrible thing he'd done. He confided in his superiors at work and gave what amounted to a naked plea for help. They said, quite sensitively, "Ted, if you had a drug or alcohol problem or gambling, or even if you deliberately threw up after lunch we have company programs to handle all that but . . . this school zone thing. That is what you said, isn't it? Some kind of school zone throbbing in your brain. I . . . We're going to have to let you go, son."

Dear Gangster: *My girl keeps telling me if I clean up my act (cut the booze and the weed) I'll be able to truly enjoy life. I tell her, I'm enjoying life just fine. She says I have to stop and face the problems that make me drink and whatnot. I got no problems, baby. There ain't nothin' eating at me. I just like to have a good time. I got no problems at work. I got money in the bank. My mama loves me. I'm not impotent.*   **—Everything Is Beautiful in My Own Way**

Dear Beautiful, Baby: I hate to keep harping on this but these people who insist everybody clean up are killing me. They are weak, they are so fucking weak. They couldn't handle drinking or drugs or whatever, they succumbed to it. We, on the other hand, keep our lives in control, get our asses up and to work every day, don't alienate our friends or family *plus* get wasted and flush out our systems at will. We are strong, so fucking strong. We really need to cut ourselves off from these people. Let this be a notice to the weak. Stay away.

SEX CAN BE A FAMILY THING

Dear Gangster: *I'm a single mom with a wonderful two-and-a-half-year-old son. My new boyfriend and I usually just stay at my place on the weekends and party late into the night because I really can't afford a sitter right now. The problem is, that by six A.M. my little boy has had about thirteen hours sleep and wakes us both up and for the rest of the day my boyfriend walks around like he's going to kill me.*
—Problem Child

Dear P.C.: O.K. This is what you do but it's not something you wanna brag about or the Health and Rehabilitative Services might come down on you. You've got to get the kid on your schedule. While you're partying you've got to force the child to keep pace with you. A friend of mine does this by feeding his son

Snoballs nonstop. At first the kid's a pain but by midnight he's just running on Snoballs—groggy, giddy, but wide-eyed. He's as happy as a puppy just gnawing on a sofa arm for a couple of hours and by one or two in the morning you're so wasted you don't even notice him. Everyone eventually passes out together in one big heap. The place will be littered with a million Hostess wrappers along with all the cigarette butts and empty beer cans but everyone can sleep till noon. And, if your son's so wonderful, twenty-five years and three wives from now he'll certainly understand why his mom did what she did and accept the fact that he'll have to lay on a couch and pay some guy $105 an hour for seven years to figure out why he gets this relentless urge to eat squishy pink igloo-shaped things at three in the morning.

Dear Gangster: *How do my wife and I bring spontaneity back to sex with the kids running around all the time?*

—**Last Sex 8/9/88**

Dear 8/9/88: You've got to use them like a sex tool. Like a vibrating bed, but without having to feed them quarters. What my wife and I like to do is be right in the middle of the act and then call the children. Scream their names. They come running, find the door locked, begin pounding fiercely and yelling "Mommy, Daddyyyyy . . ." We yell back. The whole room is in an uproar with the pounding and the whole family wailing. Then the dog starts up and the neigh-bors are phoning. It's unearthly. If you can hold on long enough one of you can hang your head over the bed upside down and have kind of an "unbearable lightness of being" moment as the children's small fingers start coming under the crack of the door and claw the carpet in desperation. What I'm saying is—sex can be a family thing.

Dear Gangster: *I married this woman. I added her name to my credit cards. I bought her a new home and an almost new car. I take her out to dinner at least once a week and all she has to say is, "You don't show me enough love." I say: I married you, I put your name on my credit cards, I . . . I don't know what she wants from me.*

—Show Me the Way

Dear Show Me: This works in degrees. You give them too much right away and they start wanting things from you that may not even exist. I've learned that you've got to go as low as you can early in a relationship so it doesn't take much to "show" gradual improvement as the years go by. Entering a relationship as Mr. Wonderful is a great concept but where you gonna go with that act? For example, if she had left her checkbook at your house after your first date and you used it to pay a few bills she'd be upset and tell all her girlfriends. Once you got past that incident though, what would you have to do to take a step up in her book? Armor All her dashboard? Take her to Sizzler? You can hear her telling her friends in the office now. "The first time we went out he stole my checkbook but yesterday he came over and Armor Alled my dash. What a sweetheart." That's why I can't encourage people enough to have an alcohol or drug problem in the first stages of a relationship. Because after a person has put up with that crap and visited you in rehab and all there's no place for you to go but up, up, up. You can coast for the rest of your life. How's Tony doing? "Oh, he's been off the crack for eight months now. He's so great. Yesterday he spent the whole afternoon high-lighting his favorite shows in the TV Guide with a yellow marker."

Now, in your case, you prince, you've put yourself in a real bad spot. I only see two options. Divorce her and start over using this "as low as you can go" method, or buy her a new car.

Dear Gangster: *When I first moved in with my boyfriend everything was fine. it was just me, him, and our Akita. But then a friend that went to school with him in Denver came to visit. That was over two and a half months ago. The guy's still here. You might think I'm upset about the guy overstaying his welcome but that's not it. He's real nice. The thing is our dog, Shelby, has really taken to him. I used to get the leaps and bounds when I came home but now he saves them for this guy. I'm jealous.* **—Puppy Love**

Dear Puppy Love: Why is it that the people who don't mind overstaying their welcome and mooching off friends always get along so well with dogs? Anyway, you probably can't get the dog to hate this guy. Dogs are such masochists. But maybe you can get the guy to take a disliking to the dog. Try putting a couple of spoonfuls of the dog's saliva in his coffee. It should rise to the top. Or you could bite him while he's sleeping. Even if you get caught and he stands up in the darkness and says, "You bit me!" you could calmly reply, "Yes, and if my dog didn't love you so much he would have done it himself." Believe me, he's waiting for something like that to happen. Vagabonds like him always wait for dramatic exits so they have a story to tell in the next town. It's a Sam Elliot thing, I think. The next morning he'll be packing his duffel bag and whistling Paul Simon's "America" as his own lullaby plays out. "Hadda leave Denver, Hadda go to San Jose, Hadda leave when a woman bit me, Hadda break a dog's heart along the way."

Dear Gangster: *I'm as worried about the environment as the next person but my husband is driving me crazy. He's constantly yelling at me for putting metal in the aluminum bin and buying take-out from this little diner that still uses Styrofoam containers. I can't take it anymore.* **—Recycle This**

Dear Recycle: You're pitiful. I'm sitting on my front steps right now watching my neighbor change the oil in his truck. His belly is sticking out just far enough so you can tickle it with a stick and run before he has time to eyewitness your shoes. Anyway, he did his wife's car about ten minutes ago and I didn't even flinch when I saw him empty the crankcase into a bowl that said "Prince" on it and the pooch came out and lapped it up. Now, I can't expect someone with your disposition to do as much as one single dog in this world, but please, get with the program.

Dear Gangster: *Gangster Guy, tell my mom she's wrong. I'm twelve years old and when I went to kiss my little brother good night on October 2, 1991, he yelled for my mom and told her I pressed my lips against his and held them there for three minutes. My mom accused me of practicing kissing on him. She said, "He's no kissing dummy." I said I wasn't doing it. No way. Was I?*

—Kissing Bandit

Dear KB: It's only natural to find some use for an annoying little brother. But believe me, that's as good as it gets with a little brother. Go back to making out with the posters on your walls. It's the same sensation.

Dear Gangster: *I was just involved in an amicable divorce with a decent guy who I happened to outgrow. He took it well enough, almost too well. And now I know why. The papers have been finalized for six weeks and he still hasn't moved out. He keeps saying, "I just need some time to think, to sort some things out in my head, and then I'll be out of your life forever." But Jesus.*   **—Hit the Road Jack**

Dear Hit: You gotta love these guys, don't you? An associate of mine is in the same kind of situation only she's not as tough as you. For months after the divorce I used to hear her over the phone: "Shoo, shoo, now Matthew. Go, start a new life. Go, sit closer to the door." I told her you just gotta kick his ass out but she claimed it wasn't really that bad. "I work fourteen-hour days," she said. "I'm too weak to be throwing people." To this day he still shows up on her patio around the holidays. He seems harmless and he's become such an adorable character because after the divorce he let his weight go and he's got this big bushy beard. I sometimes like to stop and pet him when I walk through her courtyard.

Dear Gangster: *My husband and I have only been married for nine months. I'm twenty-two and he's twenty. The thing is, we borrowed some money from relatives of mine because we got in a jam. It's no big deal really but my husband is a monster about it. We were over these people's house last Sunday and he wouldn't even let me swim in their pool. "Not until we pay the money back," he screamed. I told him, just 'cause we owe these people money doesn't mean we can't swim in their pool. They invited us over. Well, he almost smacked me for fighting about it and now he says we're not going near them until we pay off the debt.*   **—Why the Big Deal?**

Dear Why the Big?:   I know what he's hearing in his ears. "Oh yeah, they're over here swimming in my pool and they owe me money. Look at the big splash he's making. Does that look like the splash of a man that owes the person whose pool he's swimming in $1,500?" I had a similar problem with an old girlfriend's sister. We'd borrowed a chunk of money to get an apartment and were barely paying it back but every weekend the sister would invite us over. I started saying, "Now we're just going to visit. We can't stay for dinner." I'd had a couple of bad experiences like the time I thought I caught her brother-in-law glaring at me from across the room just as I was wiping some potato salad off my face and licking my fingers. I could hear his stare. "Oh, yeah, get every last speck of mayo off your fingers. Go ahead, slap on the roast beef. Why not, you owe me $1,200 and I won't have any leftover lunch meat for work this week. That's perfect, you debt-ridden piece of human garbage." At first my girlfriend thought I was just imagining it all but then she was in the bathroom all alone when she thought she saw the shower curtain move slightly and heard someone whisper, "I hope your belly's full." As time went on we tried organizing ourselves before visits. "Now, if they ask us if we want something to eat we say no," my girlfriend would say. But it wasn't that easy because they would keep asking us and one of us would finally say, "Yes, we'd like something to eat," even though we owe you a ton of money and may never pay you back. Then we'd get in an argument on the way home. "Why'd you say yes?" I'd say to her. Or "Why did you say yes?" she'd say to me. I'd say, "The way you were looking at me I thought you wanted me to" or she'd say, "The way you were . . ." So then we knew we couldn't trust the way we looked at each other so we started picking a number. Say nine. Only if they ask us nine times do we say yes. Only then do we eat the potato salad of the people who've been paying our rent for the last two months. "Deal," we'd say and then I'll be damned if they didn't ask us nine times. It was like they always knew our secret number.

Thank God. She made the best potato salad, her sister did. I don't know what kind of person this makes me but, you know, we never did pay those people back but for some reason when I think of that I don't feel guilty.

I feel hungry.

Dear Gangster: *I'm a divorced mother with two wonderful children. I've got a good job and date regularly and my only problem is* *my scuzzy ex-husband. He doesn't have a job or do anything regularly as far as I can tell, but he wants to see the children every weekend. All he does is sit around my place. He says he doesn't have the money to take them anywhere. I say, how about the park? He says, "How 'bout it?" And just sits there.*   **—How 'bout a Solution?**

Dear 'bout: A neighbor of mine was in a similar situation that seemed to work out to my advantage, if no one else's. Her ex, who is a musician, lived in his car between gigs and at first she would just leave the house when he came over and let him see them there, but then she got sick and tired of that. "Why should I have to leave my house for that scum?" she said.

Eventually, she forced him to take them in the car but the poor guy didn't even have gas money so he would only pull down the street a little ways. One day he was in front of my house and I couldn't bear to see him out there in the cold trying to play the accordion for those two youngun's in the back seat and scraping his knuckles on the steering column when he tried to hit those, what do you call them, not high notes, long notes, I guess. When he tried to hit those long notes. Anyway, what I did was give him a few bucks for gas and send him up to the 7-Eleven to get me a two-liter of Classic Coke and a round of Slurpies for the toddlers and then down to the post office and maybe by Blockbuster Video, "as long as you have the time." They stop in front of my house every week now. This way I hardly ever have to do any of my own errands and I get to help out a struggling musician/father at the same time. The kids even come skipping down early in the week to check on upcoming events. "How's the Laundromat sound, girls?" "Oh, we love it. It's so warm in there next to the dryers," they chorus.

Give me a call, maybe we can work something out with your situation.

Dear Gangster: *Is there some kind of new creature out there that just likes to toy with women? I've been seeing this thing that is sending me all kinds of mixed signals.*

—Or Maybe He's Just Married

Dear Maybe: You should know about this guy.

I'll call him Brian because that's his name and he seems proud of himself. "Yeah please, use my name," he says. "I want to know if there are other people coping the way I am."

He calls it coping but what he does—and I'm kind of interested myself if other people are doing this—is cheat on his wife without ever actually consummating another relationship.

"It started with this girl named Valerie," he says. (I changed her name because I'm not sure if she's proud of herself or not.) Valerie was a co-worker who liked to sit by the window with her back to the sun in the company cafeteria. "Just like I did," Brian says. "Only my shirt would get all sweated up but hers never did. She could really handle the midday sun."

She could handle the midday sun and she always circled parking lots till she found the perfect spot. "Sometimes it wasn't even the perfect spot," Brian says. "I mean, sometimes we'd pass a better spot and while she was looking for an even better spot she'd lose the best spot because she had to be sure it was the best spot before she settled for a spot that might not be the best spot."

Anyway, he loved this about her. That, and the way her back handled the heat and "how I got real nervous when I got too close to her."

"I hadn't felt that for a long time," he says. "Not since I met my wife."

You can see where this is headed. Happily married man meets woman at work. Finds certain qualities about her irresistible—like how she parks a car at the mall—and has an affair.

That's how I first saw it too, but there's one thing atypical about Brian's situation. He's too loyal to his wife to have sex with a woman that makes him nervous close-up.

"I could never do that," Brian says. "I could eat lunch with her a thousand times. I could return her panty hose to the drugstore across the street for her. Exchange actually. You see there was a sale and she didn't know about it till the afternoon and they had charged her regular price in the morning and she had to finish these reports. And anyway, I said I'd run over there for her 'cause I needed some . . . Listen, I draw the line at sex but . . ."

But he's only human. "So we were at her apartment," he says. I stopped him. Up until then he was nickel and dimin' me. A little hanging out in the cafeteria, circling parking lots, getting nervous in tight situations. So how the hell did he end up in her apartment?

"I told her we should go to her apartment," he says. "We both left the office on separate errands and then met there."

That sounds awfully premeditated to me.

"Yeah, that's what I wanted her to think," Brian says. I was mixed up. He didn't want to have an affair but he wanted her to think he did and . . .

"I didn't say I didn't want to have an affair," he says. "I said I couldn't have sex with her."

"So what'd you do?"

"We kissed. We kissed for a long time."

"That's it?"

"I unbuttoned her shirt."

"You . . . "

"I wanted to see them."

"You're pitiful. Was that it?"

"Well, with her."

As soon as he saw what he wanted to see he folded. "I can't

do this," he said. "I thought I could but I can't. I love my wife."
But that wasn't the end of it. He's done this with three women
since, leaving each of them in various stages of undress.

"I act like my shoe laces are stuck and before you know it
they're completely naked and I have to explain how I just can't
do it. I love my wife."

"I don't understand. Your wife would know your love is true
as long as the naked woman was just hovering above you while
you fumbled with your shoe laces and not in bed with you?"

"Don't be silly. My wife is never gonna find out about any of
this. She's got her own life. This is for my own conscience. In my
heart I know I'm not doing anything that bad. Nobody gets hurt."

"What about the other women?"

"They can put their clothes back on."

Dear Gangster: *How do I get my husband to pay more attention to me? He rarely suggests we spend time together and prefers to
eat his meals by himself with a book. He doesn't even look up from his
computer when answering a question. Any suggestions?*

—Slightly Widowed

Dear Slightly: I'm going to suggest counseling but the
only time I suggest counseling is when you know going in you're
only doing it to annoy the other party before you divorce them.
My sister had a similar problem to yours. There was just no com-
munication. So she went into the counseling with good intentions but about halfway through, when she started hearing what
was actually on his mind, she knew she wanted nothing to do
with him.

But she saw how he hated the sessions so she stayed in the
marriage an extra eighteen weeks for the sheer torture of it. She
still calls him occasionally to remind him of the counselor, "So,
what are you feeling tonight, Michael?"

Dear Gangster: *My husband and I have reached the point where, financially, we can afford to get a live-in nanny for our eighteen-month-old son. The thing is, this girl that was recommended by my husband's sister is extremely attractive and I know I'm going to feel threatened by her. Am I being foolish or is it only natural?*

—**Hazel, Where Are You?**

Dear Looking For Hazel: I hope it's not sex you're worried about because worse things can happen when you bring someone into the fold. A guy I know who barely finished high school went on to build himself a very lucrative business selling strictly expensive sink fixtures. His lack of education never bothered him until one day. One day he and his beautiful wife (who has the shape of an expensive sink fixture by the way) decided to allow a college student to move in and watch their two sons at night and on weekends. This girl was always coming home from school and babbling about all the great things going down on campus while she poured Mr. Bubble into the tub for the kids. Anyway, Sinkman gets it in his head that he always wanted to get a college degree. He started with just one class in "egg planting" or something and the next thing I heard his business was going down the drain. His wife had only been doing charity work for hospice until this happened and when they started going broke she actually asked if she could be hired on in a paying position. It gets worse. Last I heard Sinkman was in his sixth year as a full-time drama student. They're surviving on hospice wages, if that's possible. The boys are living with an aunt two counties away and the college nanny who quit school after the second semester is making a fortune selling something that was described to me as "recycled invisible garden hoses."

Dear Gangster: *I'm a thirty-five-year-old woman and have been married for thirteen years. Is lust important? If it is, how do I get it?* **—I Wanna Lust**

Dear I Wanna: Lust! What the hell is lust? You remind me of people who start wars. Where do you find the time to think about stuff like this? Why aren't you adding up your sick days and planning to call in Friday like the rest of us or trying to make up your mind whether you should pay full theater price for *The Grifters* or wait for the video. Or why don't you just admit you want out of the relationship and you're looking for an excuse. I happen to know your man is in excellent physical condition and a great barbecuer so you're just grasping for something, anything. Just go and make everyone happy. You're thirty-five, for Christ's sake. Lust doesn't have anything to do with anything. You're living in a Joey Lawrence world. Just go. Go.

Dear Gangster: *Every night my husband corrals me and says come sit by me and let's talk. But then he just stares at the TV. After a half hour I usually go call one of my girlfriends but then he gets mad. Last night the only thing he said to me was, "I think I'm gonna fix our bicycles tomorrow," and then when we went to bed he expected me to make love to him.* **—Silent Partner**

Dear Partner: What does it tell us about the state of our empire when a simple man who just wants to fix bicycles and have sex isn't appreciated? There, I said it.

Dear Gangster: *I've been reading a lot of books lately on ways to bring new life to old sex. My wife likes to read the books too, I think they turn her on, but when it comes to action she says, "Oh, don't be silly, that's too complicated." What can I do to get her to perform the tricks we only read about?* **—Ready to Perform**

Dear Ready: It's not the trick, it's the practice that gets a bit awkward. Am I the only one left who thinks basic sex is too much work as it is?

Dear Gangster: *My boyfriend thinks I've been acting kind of funny lately and the other day he asked me if there was "someone else." There isn't and I told him that. But at the same time I got this funny feeling in my gut, kind of a mixture of queasiness and elation. Like my life was suddenly full of possibilities I'm hesitant to explore. Maybe there could be someone else. Is this just something that hits you about this age?*   **—Mid-(Twenties) Life Crisis**

Dear Mid-Twenties: Is there someone else? No. But I want there to be. I don't know how many times that thought has run through my mind when I've been asked that question. You stop yourself because you know it's selfish reasoning but it's honest too, isn't it? No matter how good and safe things are you want somebody to come out of the shadows and undress the night, put the fire back on the horizon. Can I tell you a secret? There is somebody else. And can I give you some advice? Don't go looking for him.

Dear Gangster: *My husband I went to a counselor recently and he suggested that we get a tape recorder and start recording our arguments so we can listen to ourselves afterwards. I think it's a crazy idea.*   **—Testing, Testing**

Dear Testing: Not so fast. I was proud to make the acquaintance of a couple that recorded all their disputes. Before long they were planning arguments and then getting drunk and listening to them on the weekends. They would laugh so hard at themselves that they would invite the neighbors over, like you do to be polite when you're having a loud party. "Come on over and listen to us," they'd say. To make a long story longer, after the counselor listened to their tapes, and heralded them "brilliant confrontations," he asked if he could mail some out to fellow counselors for seminars. One thing led to another and pretty soon they were selling the tapes to self-help centers across the country and overseas. I'll never forget the day they said, "Come on over and listen to us . . . in Portuguese." After a while they were able to make a living at arguing. Isn't that beautiful? They're divorced now but they still get together three days a week to fight. It's strictly business.

Dear Gangster: *Do you know what it's like to wake up one day and look at someone you've been living with for six years as if they were a stranger? All of a sudden I'm looking at this guy like I don't even know him. Like I can't imagine what I'm doing with him. It's scary.*   **—Stranger in the House**

Dear Stranger in House: Not as frightening as when you do know who that person is. Did you stop to think you may be actually looking at him honestly for the first time?

Dear Gangster: *I have only been married to this lug for about six months and already he's refusing to cooperate. He's Mr. No Compromise. I tell him, "Listen, we're both starting fresh here and any rules we set up are for the both of us." But all he has to say when I try to get him to keep something organized or it's his turn to do some chore is, "Knock it off, you're not my mother." How am I going crack him?*
                    —Nobody's Mother

Dear Nobody's Mama: That reminds me of my old neighbors. Every time they argued they blasted each other with,

"You're not my mother." "Oh, yeah, you're not my father." "You're not my big sister." "Well, you're not my little brother." They must have eventually realized that neither one was so much as the other's uncle. They weren't related in any way whatsoever. So they got a divorce. Now they greet each other with big grins. "You're not my husband." "You're not my wife." Everything is beautiful.

Dear Gangster: *My husband is not a religious person, never has been. But now, each night before he goes to bed, he insists on getting down on his knees and praying for the bad lieutenant. I told him it was just a movie but he says I don't understand what the lieutenant went through. "It wasn't just a movie," he screams at me. "It was . . ." Well, he has trouble explaining it and I think he's losing it to tell you the truth.*

—Harvey Keitel is God (He Told Me to Say That.)

Dear He May Very Well Be: To tell you the truth we all lost a little to the *Bad Lieutenant* and you shouldn't speak of what you do not understand. You know, I can be nasty and when those preachers come knocking on my door I usually turn them away with a wise remark but it just so happens a group of about eight young men and women stopped by right after I had been up all night watching the *Lieutenant* several times. They said, "Can we pray for you?" I kind of shrugged. They said, "Is there anyone you would like us to pray for, a loved one?" Well, yes, I thought, and let them in. The men were wearing dark, heavy sport coats but the women wore these white, tent-like things that never seemed to touch their bodies. They had no shapes but they all had beautiful strawberry hair. When I told them I wanted to pray for the Bad Lieutenant they all kept saying, "Who? Who?" So I finally settled for Harvey. We were all about halfway through the prayer when I stood up and walked around in front of where the women were kneeling and sort of looked down the front of their tents and saw shapes.

That one was for you, Lieutenant. Rest in peace.

Dear Gangster: *My wife is driving me nutso. She has to have her little noises or she can't go to sleep. I thought people needed quiet but she's just the opposite. This week she wants the faucet dripping. Is that insane or what?* —**Drip Drip**

Dear Drip: I was involved with a women who kept adding so many sounds that I think she kept me around only to be in charge of the noise. it started out with just the overhead fan whisping but then that went out one night and she bought an oscillator and then when the other one was fixed she had to have both and then there was this cassette tape of a fire crackling that got thrown in the mix somehow and then she liked to lock the cat in the bathroom where he had this scratch board he'd claw at and I remember the night the cat was sick I had to go in there and scratch at this thing just so or she could tell I wasn't the cat. "I'm not the fucking cat," I told her but anyway I finally got it down and I remember glimpsing myself in the mirror as I strummed it like a stringless cat banjo.

I'll tell you something, 'cause I'm an honest cat, she ended up leaving me, not the other way around. I have a quiet life now and I can't even drink.

Dear Gangster: *I'm sitting in my usual chair. My wife and two-and-a-half-year-old son are frolicking on the floor with a puppy they just brought home. They're both laughing and tossing names out at me, "Should we name him Astro? Or Devo? Or Hudson? Flipper?" I laugh. I've got a magazine in my hand that's been open to the same page for about forty minutes, a Columbia House ad. I have some num-*

bers memorized. The Smithereens' "Blow Up"—428854. The Pixies' "Trompe Le Monde"—429571. It feels so strange. They haven't a clue what I'm thinking. They don't know that I plan to be gone in a week. My wife and I haven't been having any trouble but I've been having trouble. I just have to get out. I don't know how to explain it. If I did maybe I'd explain it to her. I've already got everything set. I know exactly where I'll be living and how much money I'll need to survive and how much they'll need to stay in this house comfortably. I know that I'm leaving next Thursday because that's the night we usually go to a show or dinner and my mother-in-law watches our son. After I tell her and leave, her mother will be on her way over to comfort her and the next day I leave on a business trip for two weeks to cushion myself. It's all planned so well. I won't have to see her suffer. She won't have to be disgusted by my cold responses and lack of whys. I don't know how I can sit here idly staring at a single magazine page knowing everything and she can play with a puppy in the home she loves with the child she loves and the man she loves and know nothing. It makes me wonder about myself. Nobody has to do that for me.

We're going to dinner tonight. I'll eat heartily and not because I don't want her to know anything is wrong but because I'm hungry. I'm not sweating at night and I'm not scared about leaving them behind. It's just the knowing that's beginning to bother me, don't you think? I want to enjoy that dinner tonight. I want to sleep comfortably tonight without anyone being upset. I want it to be that way every day until I leave this house. And I want to name that puppy. I want the name I blurt out to be the one everyone says, "Yeah, that's it," to. I want them to laugh and cheer and stand up and say, "That settles it. That's his name." And then I want to leave.   **—So Sure of Myself**

Dear So Sure: Jesus Jones' "Doubt"—417691.

Dear Gangster: I'm in the process of divorcing my husband. It's not really messy. We don't have any kids, just a lot of property. The *thing is, when we meet together with our respective lawyers he acts like I'm not even there. He looks at me but doesn't really acknowledge me, you know what I mean? Is this something lawyers tell their clients to do, some kind of power play or something?*

—The Invisible Woman

Dear Invisible Woman: I once stood over a table where five grown men sat trying to convince a good friend that the way to go at any proceedings is to just act like she doesn't exist. "I don't want to be mean or anything," the guy said. "I just really don't know how to act toward her in that kind of situation."

"Like she doesn't exist," his buddies all chorused. I tried to convince him that you can make believe a lot of things don't exist. You can pretend the fat man who cruises your street and tosses a newspaper on your front lawn every morning at four in the morning doesn't exist. You can make believe there isn't a ring in the cereal bowl you've been using for the past 678 mornings and only quickly rinsing in the sink. You can be oblivious to the fact that your spinal column is squeezing you slowly into a little old man. You can insist that you gave up dreaming years ago but you can never ever make believe a woman who you've lived with, slept with, breathed with, and has her name on every one of your credit cards, doesn't exist. He didn't listen. It got very messy and the last time I saw him he was going on his tenth court appearance. He looked awful. He turned his head in my direction (which seemed to take an extreme amount of effort), tossed his arms in the air (which seemed to drain the last ounce of strength out of him) and said, "She exists."

Dear Gangster: *Now that I'm divorced, my friends say: "Foster companionships; be patient; you're vulnerable; don't lose your head." Me? I long to be naked with many women. Bathe them. Mas-*

*sage them. Roll in their scent like a hound with a dead squirrel. What
first steps do you advise?*   **—Anxious**

Dear Anxious: First step: A neutering.

Let's get some perspective. Let's take high school for instance.
You weren't all that popular, were you? And the times you did
have a girlfriend, she was perfect for you. Meaning she was
about average, too. Brown eyes, brown hair, a B- average to
your C+. Girls are always a little smarter, even the average
ones. You both liked sports but neither of you had the confidence to play on a team. So you went to movies, sometimes
two or three a week, and fumbled with zippers and buttons
and got to know each other's parents. Her mother made the best
pasta, yours the best pot roast. And then you got sick of each
other.

In the nick of time, a friend of hers gave you a signal. She'd
heard you were a decent guy, so she told somebody to tell you
that she'd probably go out with you. She was about average because she used to be a friend of your last girlfriend (average people stick together). She was a little different—less baby fat around
her waist, a little more on her thighs. Your mother still made the
best pot roast, but your new girl's mother's specialty was London
broil. You adjusted.

By summer, you'd both change partners and then again and
maybe again. Meat loaf, lasagne, corned beef. Then the sex went a
step further and the person you were with at the time became
precious. Make believe "I love you's" were exchanged and you got
better at sex. The partner didn't matter. There was nothing average about this.

By the end of high school, the holding hands in front of the
parents and then sneaking sheets out the door to roll on beneath
the stars was getting tiresome. Was it the act? Was it the meat

loaf? Nobody knew, but you both cried like babies when you split up. Maybe you really did love each other.

Oh well, you've got your whole life ahead of you. You're going to college. But you find out you're even more invisible there. Everyone seems to be older than you. In fact, everyone seems to be "above average." You take a chance and approach someone without any of the adolescent antics. She turns you down politely. You try again with the one that smiled at you once. She turns you down with a smile. Finally, you fall into someone at a party after you've both had too much to drink. She picks you up off the ground. Acceptance feels good.

You find yourself out in the world and then one day it just happens. This beautiful woman looks directly at you. She's way above average. You ask the question. She says yes. You ask more questions. She keeps on saying yes. The wedding is great. No lasagne, no corned beef. The sex is great. You show her off. You lay beneath the stars.

A year goes by, maybe two, maybe five. You resist all the women coming on to you. You love your wife. Then you pick the year; maybe you both do. Everything's turning back to meat loaf. Maybe you're starting to feel the baby fat again. Maybe she's finally admitting she's too good for you. If you were free, you could go back and pluck those women you'd passed on. Freedom means no loyalty. Where do I sign?

Now it's been six months and all your friends are telling you to take it easy. That's good advice. The girls in the wings must have been in your imagination. When you think about your past, you realize there never was any string of naked women knocking at your door—there were a few sweet girls, mutual needs, some tears, and someone who was too good for you who's lost forever.

So what makes you think the parade's going to start now?

Don't make me laugh.

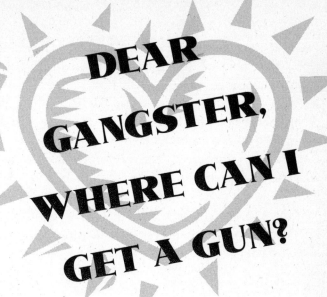

DEAR GANGSTER, WHERE CAN I GET A GUN?

Dear Gangster: *I never thought I'd feel suicidal over a woman. I always thought it a childish thing. But I've never felt this way about anyone, not even my dog. I'm pretty sure it's completely over between us. I've done the groveling and orchestrated the sponta- neous romantic tricks that I thought would win her over. I've done it all. Now it's either go on with my life or . . . not.*

—Decisions, Decisions

Dear Decisions: Suicide is never the way to go.

But, if you did decide to do it I must mention a fellow I heard about recently who, before shooting himself, put those lit- tle yellow Post-it notes all over everything at his house. When friends arrived at his door there was one saying, "I'm inside dead.

Don't bother coming back later." And inside on a box of detergent next to his body he had a Post-it that said, "This is for the cleanup. Rubber gloves are in the bottom left hand drawer in the kitchen." And all his possessions had Post-its right on them, like on his Walkman it said, "This is yours, Uncle John. Extra batteries on the bookcase." Even his hamster was tagged. "To you Greg. Don't get any crazy ideas." I never realized how handy Post-its could be. And quick. And to the point. Not a bad way to make an exit, but he was just ending it because he couldn't pay his bills or something. Something silly. To do it for love is so much more honorable. Anyway, I think you should at least postpone doing anything until you decide what the perfect . . . Oh I know, we won't put the burden on you. We'll have the readers write in. We'll have a Post-it contest. And the question is, in this situation, what would be the perfect words to scribble on the Post-it you would attach to your heart?

Dear Gangster: *Before I even knew this guy like I know him now I told him I had no intentions of ever getting married again. When we started dating I spent the whole second date talking about how I'd never get married again. When we moved in together all I could talk about was how it was so great to be able to just live together and never have to worry about whether we were married or not. I was so happy. Well, what do you think we've been arguing about for the past four months? He keeps saying, "But this is different, things are different now, I'm different, you're different." Excuse me, but nothing's changed. I'm not getting married again and I don't know how the hell to get it through this guy's head. What does it take to get a pointed point across these days?* **—No, a Thousand Times No**

Dear No: A Post-it.

Dear Gangster: *Since my fella moved out I've kinda en-shrined the three shirts he left behind. One silk and two flannels. First thing in the morning, as soon as I come home from work, and before I go to bed every night I go to them in the closet. They're wrapped in plastic and I take one out at a time. First I check the pockets, like there's going to be a note listing the real reasons he left, and then I un-button them and button them back up in a fidgety type ritual. Why can't I just take them to the dry cleaners and never pick them up?*

—Three Shirts and a Heart on Every Sleeve.

Dear Three Shirts: Do you have to dry-clean flannels? I've got to make a note of that.

I had an acquaintance who somehow ended up with chairs from her old boyfriends. I guess she insisted that each leave one chair before they moved out. Break my heart, but leave that damned recliner. She had all kinds—wicker, beanbag, La-z-Boy— and would set them up in her living room in kind of a horseshoe like a therapy session was gonna take place. Which I suppose did, but she was the only one there. She used to spend an entire evening rotating from one chair to the next and screaming memories as if it were possible to make memories even louder than they are. Sick, yet touching. She eventually killed herself.

Anyway, in your case I think you should take this to its limit, but live. Pluck the buttons one by one then swallow them and call an ambulance. After they pump your stomach and the doctor walks in with his hands cupped and says, "What the . . ." Just stop him short and say, "They are the buttons . . . from the shirts . . . of the man I loved."

I think once you've OD'd on them, had your guts drained, and said those words in a clinical setting to a certified doctor you'll be at peace and feel able to put the buttons in a jar up on a shelf somewhere. Then take those shirts to the dry cleaner. Good luck.

Dear Gang Planker: *I'm zippity-do-dah'n up and down the aisles of the grocery store when I notice this guy following me. I knew he was following me because I did one of those things like on TV where you duck into a doorway and let them pass, only I ducked behind this Orville guy popcorn display and startled him. He's kind of cute but can you trust a guy like this? Yoo hoo, can you? Can you not? Should I, should I?*   **—Ten Items or Less**

Dear Ten Items: You're pretty playful for someone who does their own shopping. I'd say he's just your basic weak personality in a brightly lit location. I had a neighbor who got stuck on this one Thursday nighter and he ended up having to shop twice a week. Once for himself and once just to get close to her. If she went for the ground chuck he reached at the same time. If she was digging for the Cherry Garcia he was right there keeping her warm during the search. Anything to brush up against her, maybe bump a little, or scrape shoes. Sometimes he'd get behind her and only feel her clothing. You know, find a spot where the cloth is bulked up a bit and there's no contact and you can get an eighth of an inch or so between your thumb and forefinger without the owner of the wardrobe being any the wiser. I've done it in elevators a couple of times myself. Once she was crouched down low reading the back of a jar of Sinatra Marinara and while he was hovering above her she popped up real fast and he got a mouth full of her hair. It wasn't like only a strand or two, which is kinda sexy, "But a whole mouthful," he said. "One minute my mouth was empty and the next it was full with the hair of a lovely women I'd been trailing in a grocery store . . . and then it was empty again." I wonder if it's the same guy. This guy's pretty cute too.

Dear Gangster: *Tell me what to do about this pitiful guy. I broke it off with him two months ago and moved out of state. Now he's* followed me here and says he doesn't want to bother me he just wants to be near me. Yeah, right.

—Being Stalked

Dear Stalked: Did you ever think maybe that's all he needs? Maybe the ending was so abrupt he just needs to be near you a little longer. When I was working in a pizza place a few years back, a guy came in with tears in his eyes one afternoon and asked if he could do something for us, anything, volunteer work. "Volunteer work, in a pizza place?" was our first response, but we were busy and I happened to be in charge that afternoon so I let the guy make some boxes. After about the third box he started spilling his guts about how his girl dropped him and she worked in the insurance office directly above the pizza parlor. He was content just to be beneath the floor she walked on. Between boxes he would spend several minutes in sort of a spiritual trance staring up at the ceiling. He was slow as hell, but then again, he was a volunteer. And an inspiration to all of us.

Dear Gangster: *This girl took me for a ride and then unloaded me like tin cans into a recycling bin. This is the first time I've ever wanted revenge on a woman. I know you're a sicko so what would you do to her first? Give me some suggestions.*

—The Revenge of the Scorned

Dear ROTS: Find some volunteer work.

Dear Gangster: *I think I'm being followed and I don't know if I mind. The guy doesn't look too bad and he seems to keep his distance. Am I as crazy as he is for not just calling the police?*

—Staked Out

Dear Staked: It is kind of flattering, isn't it? It seems like only in the old days or when we were teenagers that we simply admired someone from afar. I think it's healthy to always be infatuated with someone you'll never really approach. My brother had this thing for this one girl for about seventeen years. He pulled a sketch out the other day of her washing her car. "I'll never forget that day," he said. The guy's got a lot of days packed away that he never forgets. It's kinda sweet but I also told him it was kinda pitiful. He said, "You know, the closest I ever got was when I stood in line behind her when she was getting her license renewed. An hour and fifteen minutes and when it was her turn I just walked away. But that's the beauty, that's the sacrifice. You can love somebody and they never even have to know it. No one has to ever know it but you."

But don't be mesmerized. If you spot the pervert again, call the cops.

Dear Gangster: *I met a decent guy on a bus of all places. I introduced him to some of my girlfriends and they all seemed to like him but the next day I started getting calls. They were saying stuff like, "What's wrong with you? You can't have a serious relationship with a guy you met on a bus." Why not?* **—On the Bus**

Dear OTB: I hate to side with friends but you have to protect yourself. What if it did get serious? For the rest of your life people could accuse you of anything, whether it be stealing a jeep or abusing your neighbor's gerbils, and your character would always be in question. You could swear, "I didn't do it! I didn't do it!" until you choked on your own innocence because there would always be somebody there to say, "Hah, this coming from a woman who married a man she met on public transportation."

Dear Gangster: *A girl I'd been going out with for six months found out about a small affair I was having and proceeded to trash my apartment. She said, "And I loved you." I don't get it. What does love have to do with wrecking my stuff?* **—No More VCR**

Dear No More: Everything. I applaud anyone who turns love into the emotional twister that it is no matter what the damages. I had a great experience once when this lovely postal worker showed up at my apartment after demolishing everything an old roommate of mine owned on the other side of town. She said she heard he was still storing some stuff at my place and would I mind if she came in. For some reason I didn't hesitate for a second. Maybe it was because I know postal workers are noted for shooting down people who "just happen to be standing around." Or maybe I was just sick of his junk cluttering up my place. Anyway, she went right to it. There was a great scene where she threw a sleeping bag over the shower rod and gutted it. I got so into the power of love that I mentioned that I myself owed the guy $45 and wondered if she could give it to him. She snatched it right up and stuffed it in her mouth. But even I was amazed when she found the contact lenses and tried grounding them into the floor with her high heels. "They're so flexible," I said. "If you want to borrow my lighter maybe you could melt them." But by that time they were imbedded in her heels and she was headed for the door. What a beautiful sight. A deeply purposeful stride, a mouth full of money owed, a man's nearsightedness under spiked heels. God, I only wished I could have been the one to trigger such emotion.

Dear Gangster: *My ex took all our workout equipment. All I'm left with is half a jump rope and a step that's about as high as a can of tuna fish. She didn't even use the stuff but I guess she didn't want me* *to keep up my great figure. I never realized how much I lived for my workout.*

Dear Looking for a Girl with a Complete Home Gym: That reminds me of my neighbor, Charles. He and his wife were, like, connected at their biker shorts, always exercising together. They actually killed one of their dogs by making him run around the block with them every night. Anyway, when his wife left him he started coming around a lot (That's one good thing about a couple that exercises fanatically. They don't come by much and when they do they're going by fast enough to kill a dog.) and saying things like, "She liked to sweat more than me, you know." He got a little demented about her leaving, especially right after dinnertime because that's when they did their aerobics together in front of the TV. She had a whole collection of exercise videos. "And she took every one of them with her," he said. After about a week he asked me if I'd come by after dinner so he wouldn't have to do it alone. "Just be in the room, you don't have to hop around or anything."

"Well, as long as I don't have to hop around," I said. But now get this. This was really neat to watch. Since she had taken all the aerobics videos he would just stick any tape in for twenty minutes or so. He had an extensive collection and I'd walk in and he'd be exercisin' to like, *Goodfellas*. And there really seemed to be a certain rhythm to it. His body seemed to wince in all the right spots. His limbs seemed to laugh at all the best scenes. Well, maybe I was just into it, but I'm telling you, you haven't lived till you've seen this guy do a step workout to the last twenty minutes of *Dog Day Afternoon*.

Dear Gangster: *Sometimes you're pushed physically and sometimes you're pushed mentally and sometimes you're just pushed and sometimes you just can't take it anymore and . . . And when does a person know if he or she is capable of killing another he or she?*

—**He or She**

Dear He or She: When it's too late.

Dear Gangster: *Where can I get a gun?*

—**I Need a Gun**

Dear I Need a Gun: I love this. This is a very honest way to start the week. And as long as we're being so blunt I'd like to send a private message out to Cindi just in case she's thinking of showing her face in front of mine in the next thousand years. Cindi, you know where not to shop, you know where not to get gas, you know where not to get the best $2.39 cheeseburger in California. You know I have a very simple routine and it would not be difficult for you to stay out of my sight. Do you understand? You know I won't even need a serious weapon to finish you off. You know I took that class in Shibumi (you never should have laughed at the fact that the class cost $650) and even if you thought it was nonsense you won't think so if you step in my line of view. Do you hear me? After studying Shibumi I could kill you with a simple house key. I could kill you with the stick from a Tootsie Pop for God's sake. Oh, oh, I could kill you with your own credit card, wouldn't that be beautiful? You know how you always made fun of me for buying those big bags full of plastic combs? "Buy a real comb, cheapskate. What color's sticking out of your pocket today, Mr. Variety Pack?" I tried to explain to you that I could get a whole bag for the price of one single comb but you wouldn't stop: "Oh, what big orange teeth that one has."

Well, let me tell you something, I won't need no hard plastic black Ace to do you in. I've got a brand new multi-pack sitting in front of me right now and any one of them could do the job proudly. How'd you like to be wiped off the face of the earth by a cheap comb?

Dear Gangster: *This isn't my problem but I guess it is. My roommate's girl dropped him for reasons I don't even know and he's locked himself in his room. It's been fourteen days now. I went to see the girl and tried to convince her to at least come by and talk to him but she said, "What do you expect me to do?" I said, "Well, what do you expect me to do?" She said, "Slip some toast under the door."*

—I Don't Need This

Dear Don't Need This: Please, if space provides and you don't think it'll be too messy, put a little marmalade on there and tell him it's from all of us who aren't coming out anymore. The year's coming to an end and we won't be back next year. The pain's just too much. We're gonna sit '96 out in our rooms. Brian Wilson had the right idea, he just made the mistake of coming back out. We're not going to make that mistake. Here's to toast riding in on dustballs by the push of a helping hand. Here's to all the bright-eyed boys and girls who still think there's love out there somewhere. Here are my car keys. Take yourselves for a ride, run up the miles. God bless.

DEAR GANGSTER, ARE YOU LOSING YOUR SENSE OF HUMOR?

Dear Gangster: *I was expecting you to come across with some New Year's resolutions. What are we supposed to do, think some up ourselves?*
—Too Busy

Dear TB: I wasn't gonna bother because I've been too depressed lately but maybe it's the best time to give other people advice. We're very lucid when we're depressed. We get to see things we should never have to see. I've noticed something about myself recently . . . actually someone pointed it out to me, which is worse, and I'm not one to center on anything physical unless I feel it somehow defines much more serious flaws in one's character, or, I guess, if someone begins to point at it in broad daylight. And if that person happens to be someone you care very much about and you can't retaliate and point right back at the *same part* of her body because, in this case, it wouldn't make much sense and . . . Anyway, I don't want to get into my problems. I want to get out of them. That's my resolution, and I'm just gonna make a list here of some things I think we should try and do this year. Together.

1. *Go some place far away and let your hair return to its natural color.*
2. *Think about the one that wasn't good enough three years ago. Maybe he or she is now. Maybe it's not too late.*
3. *Men: Don't accept the beefy little breasts you acquire in your early thirties.*
4. *Women: Don't point at your man in broad daylight on what is an otherwise glorious morning and say, "Are you just going to accept those beefy little breasts without a fight?"*
5. *Call into work dead at least once every few months. Spend that day searching for someone to love while everyone else is working. Give yourself that edge and be prepared to use the opening line, "I called in dead today, want to take a ride out to the desert?"*
6. *Don't dwell on little bouncy deficiencies in your physical appearance that beautiful women are beginning to point at. Do something constructive. Make lists.*
7. *Once a week, follow someone that catches your eye. If they duck into a hotel ride the elevator with them. Get as close as you can without blowing it. In other words, never open your mouth. Then, make some sacrifices for this person. Wait in the hotel lobby for six hours in hopes they come out to get a bowl of chili and you are able to get a glimpse of them putting a spoon to their lips or delicately crushing a cracker in their bare hands. And let that be enough.*
8. *Change your answering machine message to "I'm out following somebody. I should be back in six hours or so depending on whether they come out of their hotel room for chili or not."*
9. *Don't call your mother and insist she dig up the photos of the family*

clambake you had at the shore in 1972 so you can prove to a woman how unnoticeable your breasts were at twelve.

10. Refuse to go out with anyone in your own profession. "I'm a travel agent, he's a travel agent, we met at a travel agency." You might as well have had an arranged marriage by your ancestors. Real love doesn't just happen—at conventions.

11. If you work in an office building ride the elevator for goodness sake. Stop getting in and pressing that 7 every day. Circulate (9, 12). Explore (13, 19). You can meet new people just by saying, "Hey, what do you guys do up here?" Real love does happen—on other floors.

12. If you go to the floors below yours, say, "Hey, what do you guys do down here?"

13. Get unbusy.

14. On third thought, don't give anybody a clue what floor you're on. You don't need them comin' around wantin' to know what's up or down when you've got work to do.

15. Don't dwell on elevator stops just to push the real problem out of your mind. The real problem will only play itself out in your dreams where they'll be bigger and bouncier and General Schwartzkopf will be pointing at them with a three-foot stick.

16. If you're in your early thirties keep your shirt on during sex and especially when you sit outside afterwards for an intimate breakfast in the sweet sun that so easily sheds its honest light on your bare chest and changes a sensuously memorable morning into an "I can't get this out of my freakin' mind morning." And please, after she brings it up don't sit there as if you're comfortable talking about the problem so you can show this woman how comfortable you are talking about such problems because that's the kind of man you are even though she's just pointed out that you're turning into a woman and . . .

Dear Gangster: *When I complain about something in our relationship my girlfriend always says, "Oh, you're only saying that because you hate your job." It's never us. It's always I've got something else on my mind and take it out on her. That's not the truth.*

—Tell the Truth

Dear You Wanna Know the Truth: I get into this all the time. I'll tell someone something very honest and they'll tell me, "Ahh, that's the booze talking, or that's your depression talking or that's your weight problem talking, you don't mean that." You better believe it is, man, it's all those things talkin'. It's the depression, the booze, the child abuse, the agoraphobia, carpal tunnel, who ate my Snoball, why do I have to be Mr. Gray, my dog laughs at me, talkin'—all of those things. That's me.

And don't you think for a second I don't mean what I say.

Dear Gangster: *I've been with my boyfriend for about eight months. During the first four months he was a great guy, but now he ignores me and, actually, he hardly ever calls me anymore. Plus, he puts me behind his friends and family. He tells me he loves me but then he ignores me again. Tell me what I should do?*

—Need Extra Help

Dear Extra: Where do you fit in? Somewhere between his aunt's birthday and his Thursday afternoons at the batting cage? Does he tell you he loves you right after you tell him that he's ignoring you? I mean is it, "You've been ignoring me!" followed by "You know I love you, baby." Because if you're setting up the "I love you" then you're setting yourself up for something that doesn't exist which means he's not ignoring you, you're ignoring the truth, which is, "Nobody loves you."

Dear Gangster: *Are you losing your sense of humor?*
                              —What's Not So Funny?

Dear What's Not: You're the first person that's noticed. Thank you.

Dear Gangster: *My boyfriend won't shut up. I wanted to put this nicely, but that's the truth. He gets started on some trivial thing and then won't stop. The other afternoon I had to listen to an hour's worth of details about some dinosaur that one group of scientists said was too big to stand up on its hind legs while another group said it was perfectly plausible.*
   —Standing on My Head Waiting for Him to Shut Up

Dear Headstander: Did they have circuses back then? But come on, you're not really listening to him anyway. You're thinking about that guy at work who's so beautiful and how you touched his time card the other day and it was still vibrating because he had punched in a second before you and you held it in your hands until it stopped and then you looked at your own card and saw your name, remembered who you were and how it would never work, and how he would look naked. Stop fantasizing while your old man's trying to talk big science and maybe you'd learn a thing or two. Sometimes it takes a few thousand words to illustrate something. Not everybody can cut to the heart of a matter with three simple words like, "Ice, ice, baby."

Dear Gangster: *I've got this funny feeling that I'm completely inconsequential to the opposite sex. All of a sudden I find*

women doing things in front of me that they wouldn't do in front of a
mirror in a dark closet. Why? Because they couldn't care less what I
think. I might as well be invisible or a slight obstacle in life—something
you have to walk around once in a while, something you maybe can't
park in front of. That's it, I'm the equivalent of a fire plug. And you
know what the sad part is? I'm getting used to it. Why?

—What Am I, Canned Tuna?

Dear Tuna: First, I want to thank you for not saying
chopped liver. Second, you're not the only human fire plug in
town. Actually this guy calls himself a knickknack. "I'm a knickknack on the shelf of life," he tells me. "And really dusty, so you
can't even make out what I am. I may be like a really nice snow
leopard from the Franklin Mint or I may be just like a cheap plastic Statue of Liberty with a thermometer on my stomach." He
based this on a recent encounter in a parking lot.

"It was a happy hour so it was early and the sun was still
shining. I tried to tell myself later that maybe the sun was in her
eyes but who was I kidding. Anyway, it's crowded so I had to
park about a block away and I see her about a hundred yards
ahead of me get out of her car at the same time. So I'm staring,
but that's O.K., she's in my line of vision. And then she stops in
her tracks. I'm thinking catch-up time. She reaches in her purse
and starts combing her hair. I'm thinking, she probably thinks I
won't even notice I'm so far away. She's doing a rush job on my
account. But then I'm getting closer and she turns and looks right
at me. I mean, I'm close now, and I don't know what she saw
when she looked at me but it was like my presence was dismissed
immediately. She starts giving herself a complete make-over right
in front of me. She's pinching at her hose, checking her eye-liner
in car windows. I mean, the works. She's doing a breast adjust-
ment right in front of me, evening 'em out. When she went to

snap her panty line I turned around and started running back to my car. I was never so humiliated. Getting herself ready for everybody but me, everybody but me. I could have been a sink in a ladies' room as far as she was concerned. A faucet, a leaky faucet in a turnpike restroom with a bunch of chewing gum stuck in my spigot. That's me."

Dear Gangster: *I've been seeing this waitress who moved here from North Carolina. Well, more than seeing actually. She's been sleeping in my bed for the last four months. The thing is, I'm getting this sense that something is about to happen, like we're coming to the end of some kind of cycle, but I don't know what it is. It's not me so it must be her, right? What's happening?* **—It's Not Me**

Dear It's Not Me: It's not you. I hate to just throw this at you since I know so little about your relationship but I heard the following conversation between two waitresses last Thursday night.

"He doesn't know it yet, but as soon as I got the money I'm gone."

"You're just gonna leave, like that?"

"Soon as I got the money."

"I thought he was good. I thought everything was good, hon."

"Yeah, he's good, he's good. He's good."

"Then why're you . . ."

" 'Cause I'll have the money. I'll have enough to go."

"Is this what you always do?"

"When I get enough money."

"What about the guys? Do they know what you're plannin'?"

"When I go they know."

"Is that him? Is he here to pick you up already?"

"Yeah, can you tell him I'll be a few. I have to finish up on these two tables."

"He's cute."

"Yeah, he's cute, he's cute. He's cute."

He was. But how many times do you get the chance to know where your gratuity is headed? How many times do you figure it just ends up in a Laundromat? How many times do you get to contribute to somebody's "go fund?"

I left her a big tip.

Dear Gangster: *There's something awfully wrong in this world but I just can't figure out what it is. Love seems to be so slippery—no, greasy—no, slimy. I can't get a grip on it. Can't get it in a headlock, can't make it scream for mercy. What is it that's wrong in this world? Sum it up for me, will ya?*
—Two Words or Less Would Be Good

Dear Two Words or Less: You & Me.

NOTE: *The winning words from the "What to Scribble on the Little Yellow Post-it You Adhese to Your Heart Just before Committing Suicide over the Only Person You've Ever Loved Contest" were "Maybe it will make a good ashtray."*

Dear Gangster Person: *You are human, aren't you? I guess it doesn't even matter at this point. I just want to say I've been through it all this year. Meaning every time things got ugly one of us made it uglier. Every relationship seemed like it was destined to self-destruct. I blamed everybody. I blamed myself. Now I'm blaming everybody else again. It's a cycle. I'm Miss Failed Relationships 1991 and I've nothing to be proud of.* **—Walk Me up the Runway**

Dear up the Runway: Yeah, let's all take a walk. It was supposed to be good, wasn't it? This was gonna be the year you found "the one." You were gonna chase it, run it down, slip and slide and fall right into it. It was gonna be warm.

But then the days started clicking by and every time your new lover got on top of you felt like you were being buried alive. He left on his own and then the next one left when you begged him to and if you thought about it, late at night, you couldn't tell the difference between the two. So it goes.

And by March the losses don't even seem that significant any more. No one is ripping your heart out. Each relationship leaves nothing more than a pinhole and by the end of six months you feel like you could lay out front, stick a garden hose in your mouth, and water the lawn.

It seemed like every affair was destined to last exactly seven weekends and end on someone's answering machine.

There was that one that dragged out longer because you both took a hiatus. When you went to New York on business you came back and said, "I missed you," and when he went to Dallas to see his mother he came back and said, "I missed you." Nobody called anybody a liar then. No, you waited for some petty argument down the road and then called each other liars. It's an easy way of saying goodbye.

Remember the one you cared about the most disappeared the quickest and the one you should never have gotten mixed up with caused you to sit in the house with the lights out for five days, hoping he'd stay away. Then thinking about losing the one you did care about made you sit with the lights out for five more days. A different reason, but did it change the darkness?

You can't remember holding hands with any of them but you can remember worrying about getting AIDS from all of them.

It used to be the physical was the initial turn-on but eventually it turned into an excuse to turn things off. When everything was light you loved the muscles. When things got serious they were awkward, stiff, cartoonish, revolting.

The ones that weren't smart enough for you called you stupid and the ones that were too smart did all their talking at work. You knew that if you left off the last digit when someone asked you for your phone number they would never make the extra calls to find you. Nothing's that important.

For the first time you had to ask somebody is it over? And then walk away when nobody had an answer. Was it over?

When someone said, "I love you," you looked down for a cheat sheet, you looked for the words to be inked on the palm of your hand. You should have been prepared. You shouldn't have said, "I love making love to you," on several occasions when you were unable to say, "I love you," even once honestly.

You told yourself you enjoy being alone but you can't seem to hum that tune when the words to the song are so true. "When you're alone, you ain't nothin' but alone."

And that one friend who always listened to all your problems, all your weakness, could only offer you a preoccupied stare. So you're left with the parades of silence that go up and around the corner and you struggle to see something in that silence. You push, like a kid trying to poke through the legs of a crowd of adults to see the biggest float of all, but it's already passed you by. (One of them must have been "the one.") Will you see it again? You're not a little kid and you don't have your whole life ahead of you anymore.

And crying's just not good enough anymore, is it? Not if no one hears it. Not if someone doesn't say, "Please stop crying, I'm sorry I made you cry, I never want to see you cry again."

And months and years really do matter now. Somebody's

counting. And this was gonna be the year, wasn't it? And who's gonna kiss you on New Year's Eve? Because at midnight your time is up, and baby, it's cold inside.

It was supposed to be warm.

Dear Gangster: *Good news for a change. My boyfriend and I have been on and off for about three years, but it looks like we're going to finally get married this fall. We've even set a date. Please, please, please tell me there's no need to worry, and all I should be thinking about is wedding arrangements. So much to do, I love it.*
—Hey, Hey, Hey

Dear Hey, Hey, Hey: No, No, No. I'm sorry, but I don't think it's going to work out.

Dear Gangster: *This girl asked me to move in with her. It feels good, though. It feels right. She makes me feel wonderful. Your blessings please.*   —Yeah, She Asked Me

Dear Yeah, She Asked Me: I'm trying to picture it. The two of you cheerfully moving your possessions in. Things dropping on the walkway, and the both of you reaching to pick them up at the same time and knocking heads and laughing and tumbling on to the lawn and sending out for pizza while you both dust off your soccer trophies for their new spot over her TV. I'm even trying to picture this thing you call wonderful. But I just don't see it—none of it, not the moving day or the head-knocking or the pizza. I can't even see you finding that number for the pizza place, even though she always keeps it right by the phone. I just can't picture any of it happening.

No, I just don't see it.

Dear Gangster: *Guess what? Everything is great. The guy I've been going with for eighteen months is still the same guy I met eighteen months ago. He's caring, unselfish, warm, and funny. To tell you the truth, I don't see him ever changing. Not even after twenty-four months. I think I can stop looking at the calendar. Don't you?*
                                    —On a Month-to-Month Basis

Dear Month-to-Month: For some reason I don't see him never changing. I hesitate to pick a number—thirty-six months maybe. But if I put those months into years, it's three, and for some reason I don't see him going three years between changes. No, I just don't see it.

Dear Gangster: *My girl is giving me a second chance, and I'm holding on. I'm keeping everything in check. I know I can be good for her. I know I can do it. Don't you think a second chance is all most of us need?*   **—One More Try**

Dear One More: No.

Dear Gangster: *I've made a commitment, and it feels excellent. Making a commitment always seemed unnatural to me until I wanted it. Once made, don't you think our commitments can be as strong as our wants? Isn't it only natural?* `          `   **—Committed**

Dear Committed: No.

Dear Gangster: *There's this new girl at work, and I think that if . . .*

Dear . . . : No.

Dear Gangster: *There is a God. I've finally found the one person who . . .*

Dear . . . : No.

Dear Gangster: *Love, I mean if it's real love, does last for-ever doesn't it?*
                                        —I Mean Real Love

Dear Real Mean Love: No. But maybe it's just me.

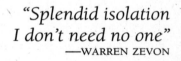

EPILOGUE

RESEVOIR DAYS, OR, A HAPPY ENDING

> *"Splendid isolation*
> *I don't need no one"*
> —WARREN ZEVON

This was the first time in ten years I was going to take my vacation all in one block. Two solid weeks—just me and what's her name. If that's not a commitment I don't know what is.

And then when she hit me with news she was almost giddy, bubbly, like a go-go dancer who'd just gotten out of the cage after a twelve-hour shift. "I love to pop into people's lives," she said, "And I really love to pop out of them."

Pop.

I could have gone to my boss and said, "You know that vacation I've been yappin' about for the past five months, the one I begged for, the one I've been dreaming about, the one I've been seeing two feet in front of me like I got a prototype virtual reality headset strapped on? Yeah, that one. Well, never mind."

I could have spent the first week trying to get her to change her feelings and maybe we'd at least get one good week in but I did that last week and the one before that.

No, I'm takin' it. And I'm spending it by myself, in my house, with absolutely no contact with the outside world. I don't need it.

DAY 1, 11:20 A.M.: People are still calling me. They want to know what I'm doing tomorrow, next Thursday afternoon, and May 17. Nothing. Absolutely nothing.

DAY 1, 1:20 P.M.: Marty called to tell me this isn't a good idea. "Your place isn't big enough to hide out in," he said. I told him square feet can't even stop me. I'm on a whole 'nother level. I'm moody, brooding, sulking, I'm like an artist now. "All you need now is some talent," he said.

DAY 1, 5:10 P.M.: I've been up for seven hours and already all the calls have stopped. That's the kind of friends I have—seven-hour friends. That's about as long as they hold up in this town. See, this was a good idea. A cleansing of acquaintances has already taken place.

DAY 1, 5:35 P.M.: I can cook. I'm just not hungry.

DAY 1, 8:15 P.M.: Just tinkering around the place, a lot of stuff I haven't played around with lately. There's that professional auto buffer my friend left here about six weeks ago. Maybe later in the week I'll go out after everyone is asleep and wax up a few of the neighbor's vehicles. A couple people will notice the shine but won't be quite sure what it is. Perhaps there's finally some toxin in the air that not only slowly kills you but puts a glistening finish on your car overnight, they'll think. Yeah, that'll be good. I'll be the Midnight Waxer.

DAY 2, 12:05 A.M.: Couldn't sleep so I took some Nyquil. Think I threw a muscle in my neck. I had tossed my head back real fast, like I was kicking down a shot of Johnny Black. Ahhhh, man, it's killin' me.

DAY 2, 12:53 A.M.: God, that's got to be some kind of record of failure for Nyquil. Forty-five minutes. I'm sure I could have gone out for forty-five minutes on my own. I mean if I just wanted to sleep for forty-three minutes I never would've even cracked the seal. I . . .

DAY 2, 1:36 A.M.: See, I slept another forty-three minutes with no help at all. I like being in full control.

DAY 2, 3:10 A.M.: It's just the neck keeping me up. I could use a little massage. No, no, not from her. I mean, I used to let her massage my neck but she sucked at it. She was all nails. And they were fake. When I was driving to work one day I felt this pain and I reached back and actually pulled a fake nail out of my neck. It was imbedded in there like a thorn.

DAY 3, 9:15 A.M.: I'm not going to wash my hair. I heard that if you don't wash your hair for days it'll come out real fluffy when you finally do. I wanna try that.

DAY 3, 12:15 P.M.: I can make a simple sandwich. There's nothing so goddamn hard about that. I'm just not hungry.

DAY 3, 2:10 P.M.: Gary called. At least I have one good friend. Not all friends self-destruct after seven hours. I'm gonna remember who my real friends are. "I need the buffer back," he said. "I'm moving to Massachusetts at the end of the week." He asked me to please leave it out in the carport so he wouldn't have to bother me. Finally people are getting the message. You got it. Don't bother me.

DAY 4, 1:10 A.M.: Called a couple of people I know and hung up when they answered. Thought it would help me sleep.

DAY 4, 2:30 A.M.: This is what it's all about. Getting up at 2:30 in the morning to watch a flick. I rented *Reservoir Dogs* on Friday and never got around to bringing it back. I'm gonna watch it in reverse this time 'cause at the end absolutely everyone in the film is dead so this way at the end everyone will be absolutely alive and have only me to thank.

DAY 6, 10:10 A.M.: Slept through day 5. When I woke up Harvey Keitel was frozen on the screen with his hands around the throat of a guy that looked like a Joe Pesci blow-up doll. I think it was Chris Penn. At least they were both still alive.

DAY 6, 11:20 A.M. Was that the phone?

"OooGA Chukka, OooGA Chukka, OooGA Chukka, I can't stop this feelin' deep inside of me"

Week 2

DAY 8, 7:54 A.M.: It works. A fluffy hair day.

DAY 8, 11:20 A.M.: I've got like this image of something trapped in my head. It's like in *Close Encounters of the Third Kind* when he can't get that shape out of his mind. I don't know what it is.

DAY 8, 1:00 P.M.: Came across tub of Cool Whip while cleaning the fridge. I bought it the first night I made dinner for her. Things went so well we never even made it to dessert. I never even cracked the seal. I don't see any reason to now. I held it up to the light and then put it back.

DAY 8, 2:30 P.M.: My horoscope says "All your favorite relatives are coming to visit." Who the hell has favorite relatives?

DAY 8, 5:35 P.M.: Video store called about Reservoir Dogs. Want to know when I'm going to bring it back. I've had it for ten days now. "It's taking a long time to rewind," I said.

DAY 8, 9:44 P.M.: I think I'll watch *Reservoir Dogs* again. I fast forward to the part where they're discussing their code names before the heist. Everybody is a color: Mr. Blue, Mr. Black, Mr. Green. Mr. Pink is pissed off. He doesn't want to be Mr. Pink. Mr.

White laughs at him. "Sure, you can laugh," Mr. Pink says. "You're a cool color."

DAY 10, 10:30 A.M.: What happened to Day 9?

DAY 10, 11:54 P.M. I'm wide awake. I know I'm wide awake. This isn't a dream. There's a man-boy standing in the middle of my bedroom wearing a Members Only jacket. Ghost? This has to be a dream.

DAY 11, 9:10 A.M.: This is scary. Now, I'm beginning to wonder if this idea to stop participating in life maybe wasn't such a good one. It's tan and it's all wrinkled like it might have been stuffed in a closet for eleven years but it's definitely real. It's just lying right there in the hallway now. I can see the little tag: Members Only. I'm afraid to touch it.

DAY 11, 2:45 P.M.: Pick up Members Only jacket with a stick.

DAY 12, 2:10 A.M.: Mr. Pink wants to be Mr. Purple. The boss says, "No. That color is already taken."

DAY 12, 3:40 A.M.: Watching a TV movie about two women who are going to stop the nuclear destruction of the world with two shotguns. They are naked except for ammunition belts. The commercials during this movie all have to do with buying 2,500 feet of a rain forest that will be preserved in your name. I call the 800 number and inquire about it. I ask if it's like a square plot, like something I could build on someday. "Or is it like 2,500 feet in a straight line, like a borderline perhaps?" Imagine owning a borderline. She's not sure. She's going to call back.

DAY 12, 1:00 P.M.: Broke the seal on the Cool Whip. Don't know what came over me but I dug my hands right into it and started sculpting. When I finished and stepped back about five paces I realized what I'd done. I know what that shape I couldn't get out of my head is. It's her nose. She has a wonderful nose, I have to give her that. I went to get a pencil to poke in some nostrils. I want them to be perfect.

DAY 12, 1:45 P.M.: Rain forest lady calls back. Hasn't got the details yet but wants to let me know she hasn't forgotten me.

DAY 13, NOON: Ordered pizza and put the tip money inside the Members Only jacket. "A lot of money. But the jacket goes with it." The delivery girl smiled like she understood and took it without discussion.

DAY 13, 3:05 P.M.: Ujena swimsuit catalog came in the mail. Took up most of the afternoon.

DAY 13, 4:40 P.M.: Carol from work calls. Wants to know which office I'll be working in on Monday. I said I wasn't so sure I'd be coming back on Monday. "What do you mean? Your vacation's up," she said. "Up, up, up." But what about next year's? I asked. Is there any way I could just slap next year's right on to the tail of this one? "Well," she said, "it's not like we really need you or anything. I'll look into it." Take your time, I said.

DAY 13, 5:05 P.M.: I want to be Mr. Gray. I wonder if that's taken.

DAY 14, 2:36 A.M.: I was tossing and turning heavily when the phone rang. I am now the proud owner of my very own borderline.

"I said, 'Doctor, ain't there nothin' I can take?'"
—"Coconut," Nilsson

Week 3

DAY 15, 9:20 A.M.: I'm not going to the bathroom today. I've gone through agony many a time holding it in when there wasn't one available but this time it's right there and I'm not going to use it. I'm turning the tables on nature.

DAY 15, 10:30 A.M.: Trying to draw my signature. Was reading about a guy who was illiterate so he learned to draw his signature. Not write it, draw it.

DAY 15, 2:00 P.M.: Work called. They were very business-like. Said my vacation for 1995 was approved for use in 1994. Was I going to use up just one week or two? I asked them if we could take this one week at a time. Said they'd check and call back.

DAY 15, 11:45 P.M.: Decided I'm not going to go to the bathroom tomorrow either.

DAY 16, 3:10 A.M.: Thought I heard something.

DAY 16, 4:05 A.M. You know she wasn't even that good-looking. She was marginally pretty, kinda like the girls who make auto parts deliveries. You know how they look kind of attractive in those little pickup trucks? That was her.

DAY 16, 10:10 A.M.: Put *Reservoir Dogs* on just so I could make an audio cassette of the last song they play while the credits roll. Put it in the Walkman so I can take it everywhere I go, even though I'm not going anywhere. "Brother bought a coconut, bought it for a dime . . ."

DAY 16, 10:15 A.M.: It takes till the third week to really get into hiding out. I'm into it. I think I'll have a beer.

DAY 16, 1:30 P.M.: I'm acting like I'm drawing my name but I know I'm really writing it, don't I?

DAY 16, 3:40 P.M.: Video store called about *Reservoir Dogs* again. I asked them how much I owed in late fees now. "Thirty-four dollars," they said. Can I just put that towards the purchase of the video, I asked. "No," they said. You mean, even if I buy it I still have to pay the late charges? "Yes."

DAY 16, 6:05 P.M.: I have to go to the bathroom.

DAY 16, 6:11 P.M.: I still have to go to the bathroom.

DAY 16, 6:15 P.M.: I'm not going. I'm not. My pledges mean something. I'm gonna think about something else.

DAY 16, 6:16 P.M.: She never shaved her legs. "My mother never had to either," she said. So there wasn't a nick or a cut on them. All seventy-eight inches (she had me measure them once, I forget the reason) were completely aerodynamic. Never had to shave them. That was great. But she bragged about it, so maybe it wasn't so great, or at least she wasn't even if her legs were. Does that make sense? God, I gotta go bad.

DAY 16, 6:30 P.M.: Kid from video store called again. WhatisitIreallycan'ttalkrightnow, I said. "Man, you sound like you have to go to the bathroom," he said. IdobutIcan'tImadeapledge. "A pledge?" he said. Whatisit?Whatisit? I said. "Well, the manager says we have your credit card slip on file so if you want to buy *Reservoir Dogs* right now you can. And if you do he won't charge you a late fee for today."

Hewon'tchargemealatefeefortoday? "Right." Deal.

DAY 16, 6:35 P.M.: It passed. Just like that it passed. I didn't think I had it in me. Musta helped to talk about it. Or maybe it's the Yoda in me. I'm in the zone, aren't I? I may never go to the bathroom again. Certainly not tomorrow.

DAY 17, 9:45 A.M.: UPS lady is at the house across the street. I know nobody is home. She's gonna need a signer. I race over and then stop in my tracks. Your shorts, I said, they're not brown. "I didn't feel like wearing all brown today," she said. You can do that I asked. But anyway, would it be O.K. if I put my name on that? I live right across the street. "Sure," she said. I took my time. She could see I was putting a lot of care into it. "Well, what do you think?" I said. "Do you think I wrote that or drew it. Come on, whatdaya think? You have to shave your legs, don't you?"

DAY 17, 12:15 P.M.: Denny from work called. "What the hell are you doing?" he said. "You're using next year's vacation to hide out in your house. You let a woman do this to you. What are you crazy?" I haven't gone to the bathroom for three days now, I said.

DAY 17, 12:16 P.M.: "Ain't there nothin' I can take? I said, 'Woo, Woo, to relieve this belly ache.' I said, 'Wah, Wah, ain't there nothin' I can take?' I said, 'Yah, Yah, . . .'"

Week 4

DAY 21, 10:11 A.M.: The Members Only jacket is back. The money I put in the pockets for the pizza girl is long gone but the jacket was laying outside on the doormat this morning. I stepped in it.

DAY 21, 1:45 P.M.: I don't know if it's because of too much beer or not going to the bathroom or what but I can't find my kneecaps. Or my elbows. I'm all puffy. I have no joints. I'm all round and squishy. I'm a man with no definition.

DAY 22, 8:15 P.M.: Next time somebody asks me if I mind if they smoke while I'm eating I'm going to mind. I keep saying, "No, I don't mind." That's going to stop. I just have to figure out how I'm going to say it now. "Do you mind if I smoke?" Yes, yes I do. But that sounds so firm. Maybe, "Well, yeah, I guess I do." That would sound like I was kind of thinking about it for the first time. That would be good, right? But I wouldn't want the person to think they were the first one I said no to. How about just "Please, don't."

DAY 22, 8:30 P.M.: She didn't smoke. But that's not why I was infatuated with her. She was special. I mean, it wasn't just physical. All her joints were visible, sure, but nothing was chiseled to perfection. I remember there was a thinness to her skin, almost a transparency. I thought I could see her heart. And there was a spirit there that didn't overwhelm but seemed to take you inside. I got inside her spirit somehow. Was it mean of her to let that happen? Did she do it on purpose? Either way I've got to let go. I'm going to say her name aloud one last time and then just let go for good.

DAY 22, 8:31 P.M.: I can't remember her name.

DAY 23, 12:05 A.M.: YES! I mind.

DAY 23, 3:33 A.M.: You know what not going to the bathroom

for days is really like, I mean after you get used to the bending over in pain and seeing spots and all that? It's like getting high and going through withdrawal at the same time. Very unique.

DAY 23, 9:22 A.M.: I'm not going to watch *Reservoir Boys* today. Last time I turned it off everyone was still alive. Let's keep it that way.

DAY 23, 11:40 A.M.: There's this country singer that looks just like her. I'm going to transfer my obsession right to her.

DAY 23, 11:42 A.M.: I'm going to buy all her albums and a gun.

DAY 23, 12:00 P.M.: I keep hearing this argument in my head between me and Richard Gere over who's going to drive the Dalai Lama to the airport. Gere is adamant. He's calling me an asshole.

DAY 23, 12:36 P.M.: There's a knock on the door. I don't know whether to peek or just throw the door open. I'm tired of peeking. "You're an asshole for saying asshole when the Dalai Lama is right in the other room," I said grabbing the door handle.

DAY 23, 12:36 P.M.: "Hi."

She had the Members Only jacket in her hand. "Is this yours?"

"No, a ghost left it here."

"I'm Claire," she said. "We're co-workers now. I started Monday. They had a bunch of stuff they needed you to sign and it's my half-day so I said I'd just pop in on you and take care of it."

Pop.

"They didn't get you to replace me, did they?" I said.

"No, no. I'm not even sure what it is you do. A couple of people have told me but I still don't understand," she giggled.

"You giggled," I said.

"Yeah, I do that instead of laugh," she said proudly, putting down the stack of papers and twirling around the room.

"Is it O.K. if I draw my name on these instead of sign them?"

She giggled and walked over and picked up the case to *Reservoir Dogs*. "This was great, wasn't it?" she said.

"It was great the twelfth time," I said. "I don't know what it is now."

"My ex-boyfriend thought it . . ."

"Why do I love the sound of that coming out of your mouth? My ex-boyfriend."

"Believe me, I love the sound of it, too."

"You want something to eat or drink? I'm all out of Nyquil but I could get you a beer or something."

"Only if you let me open it myself," she said.

"Can I ask you something?" I said not waiting for an answer. "Do you always dress like hell?"

"No, I was on my way to do my wash and I hate to wear anything that I would normally wear 'cause then all my clothes wouldn't be clean. This is my dry-the-dog and do-the-wash outfit."

"Hey, you wanna do your wash here?" I blurted. "I mean, I know you'd like to be down at the 'mat basking in the heavy air and listening to zippers bang their heads on the glass but . . ."

"Sounds good," she said.

And then I just froze and stared at her for what seemed an eternity.

"What, what is it?" she snapped me out of it.

"It's just, it's ju . . . , it's just that I thought there wasn't going to be a happy ending. I thought everybody was going to be dead at the end. Everyone is going to be disappointed."

FOR THE BEST IN PAPERBACKS, LOOK FOR THE

In every corner of the world, on every subject under the sun, Penguin represents quality and variety—the very best in publishing today.

For complete information about books available from Penguin—including Puffins, Penguin Classics, and Arkana—and how to order them, write to us at the appropriate address below. Please note that for copyright reasons the selection of books varies from country to country.

In the United Kingdom: Please write to *Dept. JC, Penguin Books Ltd, FREEPOST, West Drayton, Middlesex UB7 0BR.*

If you have any difficulty in obtaining a title, please send your order with the correct money, plus ten percent for postage and packaging, to *P.O. Box No. 11, West Drayton, Middlesex UB7 0BR*

In the United States: Please write to *Consumer Sales, Penguin USA, P.O. Box 999, Dept. 17109, Bergenfield, New Jersey 07621-0120.* VISA and MasterCard holders call 1-800-253-6476 to order all Penguin titles

In Canada: Please write to *Penguin Books Canada Ltd, 10 Alcorn Avenue, Suite 300, Toronto, Ontario M4V 3B2*

In Australia: Please write to *Penguin Books Australia Ltd, P.O. Box 257, Ringwood, Victoria 3134*

In New Zealand: Please write to *Penguin Books (NZ) Ltd, Private Bag 102902, North Shore Mail Centre, Auckland 10*

In India: Please write to *Penguin Books India Pvt Ltd, 706 Eros Apartments, 56 Nehru Place, New Delhi 110 019*

In the Netherlands: Please write to *Penguin Books Netherlands bv, Postbus 3507, NL-1001 AH Amsterdam*

In Germany: Please write to *Penguin Books Deutschland GmbH, Metzlerstrasse 26, 60594 Frankfurt am Main*

In Spain: Please write to *Penguin Books S. A., Bravo Murillo 19, 1° B, 28015 Madrid*

In Italy: Please write to *Penguin Italia s.r.l., Via Felice Casati 20, I-20124 Milano*

In France: Please write to *Penguin France S. A., 17 rue Lejeune, F-31000 Toulouse*

In Japan: Please write to *Penguin Books Japan, Ishikiribashi Building, 2-5-4, Suido, Bunkyo-ku, Tokyo 112*

In Greece: Please write to *Penguin Hellas Ltd, Dimocritou 3, GR-106 71 Athens*

In South Africa: Please write to *Longman Penguin Southern Africa (Pty) Ltd, Private Bag X08, Bertsham 2013*